John Noble Coleman

The Book of Job

Translated from the Hebrew with notes explanatory, illustrative, and critical

John Noble Coleman

The Book of Job
Translated from the Hebrew with notes explanatory, illustrative, and critical

ISBN/EAN: 9783337317980

Printed in Europe, USA, Canada, Australia, Japan

Cover: Foto ©Lupo / pixelio.de

More available books at **www.hansebooks.com**

TRANSLATED FROM THE HEBREW

WITH NOTES EXPLANATORY, ILLUSTRATIVE,
AND CRITICAL.

BY THE

REV. JOHN NOBLE COLEMAN, M.A.

LATE INCUMBENT OF VENTNOR.

LONDON
JAMES NISBET AND CO., 21 BERNERS STREET
1869.

EDINBURGH: T. CONSTABLE,
PRINTER TO THE QUEEN, AND TO THE UNIVERSITY.

PREFACE.

Bishop Warburton thus facetiously expresses himself in a letter to Dr. Hurd :—" Poor Job ! it was his eternal fate to be persecuted by his friends. His three friends passed sentence of condemnation upon him, and he has been executed in effigy ever since. He was first bound to the stake by a long catena of Greek Fathers ; then tortured by Pineda ; then strangled by Caryl ; and afterwards cut up by Wesley ; and anatomised by Garnett. I only acted the tender part of his wife, and was for making short work of him. But he was ordained, I think, by a fate like that of Prometheus, to lie still upon his dunghill, and to have his brains sucked out by owls."

Almost innumerable, indeed, have been the treatises, both in English and in foreign languages, published on the Book of Job, comprehending translations, commentaries, expositions, paraphrases, dissertations, etc. Of these, many are voluminous and lengthy. Witness the bulky tomes of Pineda, Caryl, and Wesley. One cause of this prolixity is the introduction of extraneous, irrelevant, conjectural, and supposititious matter, for which the Divinely inspired original affords little or no sanction. This remark especially applies to the published dissertations concerning the places of residence of Job and his three friends, the first subject to be considered.

THE SCENE OF THE POEM :
THE PLACES OF RESIDENCE OF JOB, ELIPHAZ, BILDAD, AND ZOPHAR.

That Job was an Idumæan Arab has the authority of Augustine. That he was an Arabian emir or sheikh,[1] "one great beyond all the

---

[1] Dr. Hales, in his *Chronology*, computes the reign of Nimrod in Shinar to have commenced in the year 2554 B.C., and the trial of Job to have occurred in the year 2337 B.C.,

sons of the East," has the general consent of antiquity, and conclusive internal evidence. But what know we of the original boundaries of ancient Idumæa, or of the original bounds of Arabia Petræa, Arabia Deserta, or Arabia Felix? Who can define the exact and precise localities of Uz, of Teman, of Shuah, of Naama? Ably has Bishop Lowth stated, that the solution of these questions is an impossibility. "Cum valde incerta sunt ea omnia, quæ ex Græcorum monumentis et Geo-

that is, 217 years after the BEGINNING of the reign of Nimrod. Now, if we bear in mind that Nimrod built four cities on the banks of the Euphrates, Babylon, Erech, Accad, and Calneh, and subsequently four cities on the banks of the Tigris, Nineveh, Rehoboth, Calah, and Resen, whensoever, wheresoever, or howsoever Nimrod may have died, he must have lived to such an advanced age, according to this computation, so as to have been contemporary with Job. It is commonly supposed, from the expression "Cush begat Nimrod," that Nimrod was a SON of Cush. This is a palpable error. Cush begat five sons, and five sons only, namely, Seba, Havilah, Sabtah, Raamah, and Sabtecha (Genesis x. 7). Nimrod was a DESCENDANT from Cush, but not a SON of Cush. Cush was the ANCESTOR of Nimrod, but not his father. As in the genealogies of Christ, detailed in Matthew and Luke, some generations are omitted according to Jewish usage, so is there an omission of one or more generations between Cush and Nimrod in this patriarchal genealogy. Without expressing any opinion on the chronological computation of Dr. Hales, it is self-evident that, as Nimrod was a DESCENDANT from Cush, not a SON of Cush, he was contemporary with Peleg. Hence it is at least probable, if not certain, that Job and Nimrod were living on the earth some portion of their lives at the same time. Now, if THE EAST include Mesopotamia, as undoubtedly it did (Genesis xxix. 1, and Numbers xxiii. 7), it may be asked, in what sense could Job be great beyond all the sons of the East during the reign of Nimrod? The solution is easy; Nimrod, the leopard-tamer (see Hislop's *Two Babylons*), the first potentate that reigned after the deluge, the avowed enemy of the triune Jehovah, came from the land of Ham. In physiognomy he was a negro, as is apparent from the figure of Nimrod from the palace of Khorsabad in volume ii. page 387 of Fairbairn's *Bible Dictionary*, and from the figure of the negro-featured Osiris or Nimrod in page 62 of Hislop's *Two Babylons*. Nimrod ruled over the sons of the East, but was not himself a son of the East by extraction or physiognomy.

Moreover, if Job and Nimrod were coevals, and if the deification of Nimrod after death was the groundwork of Babylonian idolatry, it is patent, that this idolatry must have been unknown to Job, and could not have been named or referred to in the Book of Job. Hence the only idolatry named by Job (xxxi. 26) is Sabeism, or the adoration of the sun and moon, the origin of the Carthaginian worship of Baâl Hamman and Tanith pen-Baal, as exhibited in eighty-eight votive tablets, now in the British Museum, brought by Captain Davis from Carthage, and published by Mr. Vaux of the British Museum.—See also "Religion Carthaginois" in vol. i. p. 131 of *Histoire Ancienne*, par Charles Rollin.

graphiæ longe recentioris scriptoribus Eruditi congesserunt, ad indicandam Jobi cæterorumque, qui hic memorantur, patriam et sedes; aliam prorsus rationem ineundam censeo, et ex Sacris Literis unice petendam hujusce quæstionis solutionem." The imagery of the Poem, not ancient geography, sheds the only attainable light on the scene of the Book of Job.

> VI. 15, 16.—" My brethren have dealt deceitfully as a wady,
> Like wady-streams they have passed away.
> They flow turbid by reason of the ice,
> The snow foams above them."
>
> IX. 30.—" Should I wash myself in SNOW-WATERS,
> And cleanse my hands with alkali."
>
> XXIV. 19.—" Drought and heat consume the SNOW-WATERS,
> So does Sheol those who have sinned."
>
> XXXVII. 6.—" Behold! He proclaimeth to the snow: Be thou."
>
> XXXVIII. 22.—" Hast thou entered into the stores of SNOW?
> And hast thou beheld the stores of hail?"

Now this imagery of snow-waters swelling the torrents of the Arabian wadys, and of stores of snow or snow-capped mountains, must have been unintelligible to all who were not conversant with inundations of snow-waters, and with snow-capped mountains.[1] The nearest snow-capped mountains to ancient Idumæa, or to the north-western extremity of Arabia, whatever their respective boundaries may have been, were the mountain peaks called Jebel Esh-Sheikh[2] or Mount Hermon, Jebel Sunnin, and Jebel Mukhmal.

[1] The following anecdote will show that Job and his three friends must have been intimately acquainted with snow-capped mountain-peaks, glaciers, and snow-waters. The author's revered relative, John Noble, Esquire, Alderman of Bristol, had a black man-servant from the West Indies, who had never seen snow. When for the first time he witnessed a fall of snow in Bristol, he rushed to his master, and shouted at the top of his voice: "Sugar, master; sugar, master!"

[2] "The southern portion of Anti-Lebanon slightly trends still further towards the south-west, and rises south of Rasheiya into the lofty peaks of Jebel Esh-Sheikh, the MOUNT HERMON of Scripture, the highest of all the Syrian mountains, estimated at more than 10,000 feet above the sea. It is sometimes called also Jebel el-Telj, or snowy mountain. Both its eastern and western sides are steep and uninhabited. IN THE RAVINES AROUND THE HIGHER OF THE TWO PEAKS, SNOW, OR RATHER ICE, LIES DURING THE WHOLE YEAR; and hence in summer

"Hermon (the loftiest peak of anti-Lebanon) is conspicuous from all parts of the Holy Land. Its hoary top may plainly be seen from the mountains of Samaria, from the maritime plain of Tyre, from the valley of Esdraelon, from the summit of Tabor, and even from the depths of the valley of the Dead Sea."—Fairbairn's *Bible Dictionary*. Hermon is also visible from the rivers and plains of Damascus. Hence we infer that Uz, and Teman, and Shuah, and Naama were situated to the south-east, or more probably to the east, rather than to the direct south of Judæa, because these places would thereby be in closer proximity to Hermon, Sunnin, and Mukhmal—that the location of the residences of Job and his three friends was in the north-western extremity of ancient Arabia, at no great distance from Mount Hermon—and that possibly Hermon may have been visible in the distance from one or more of their houses. That Job and his friends lived somewhere to the EAST of the snow-mountains Hermon, Sunnin, and Mukhmal, receives corroboration from the inspired declaration, "that he was great beyond ALL THE SONS OF THE EAST."[1] This expression comprehends the countries directly EAST of Judæa, and also those which were situated to the NORTH-EAST and NORTH thereof, but is never employed to designate any land SOUTH of Canaan.

"Job was not a Hebrew, but a Gentile. Job was a patriarch, a

the mountain presents at a distance the appearance of radiant stripes descending from its crown. IN THE FOURTH CENTURY THE SNOWS OF HERMON WERE CARRIED TO TYRE IN SUMMER AS A LUXURY."

"The northernmost peak rises south-east of Tripoli, and is known on the coast as Jebel Mukhmal. Its elevation is given at 8400 Paris feet. Then follows, after a long interval, Jebel Sunnin, north-of-east from Beirut, generally regarded as the highest point of Lebanon. The usual estimate of its elevation is from 9000 to 10,000. IN THE RAVINES AROUND BOTH THESE SUMMITS, SNOW IS FOUND DURING THE WHOLE SUMMER; AND FROM SUNNIN IT IS CARRIED AWAY ON MULES TO SUPPLY BEIRUT WITH A LUXURY."—Robinson's *Physical Geography of the Holy Land*. See also Robinson's *Palestine*, vol. iii. pp. 546, 547.

[1] "THE EAST denotes not only the countries which lay directly east of Palestine, but those also which stretched toward the north and east—Armenia, Assyria, Babylonia, Parthia, as well as the territories of Moab, Ammon, and Arabia Deserta."—Fairbairn's *Bible Dictionary*. "THE SONS OF THE EAST, that is, the Bedouin Arabs in the deserts east of Palestine."—Gibb's *Gesenius*. "FILII ORIENTIS sunt incolæ Arabiæ Desertæ, quæ ab oriente Palestinæ ad Euphratem protenditur."—Gesenii *Thesaurus Philologicus*.

prophet, and a priest, not of the Mosaic dispensation, but of the universal family of man. The utterances of this Book, concerning doctrines of supernatural truth, are not from Mount Sinai, or Mount Sion, but are like echoes of the oracles of God Himself conversing with man in Paradise."—*Bishop Wordsworth.*

THE AGE OF THE WORLD
IN WHICH JOB, ELIPHAZ, BILDAD, AND ZOPHAR LIVED.

The Book of Job presents to the reader a proximate clue to the age of the world, when Job flourished, apart from all conjectural supposition. This Poem has no reference to the ten plagues inflicted upon Pharaoh and the kingdom of Egypt, the Exodus, the miraculous transit of the Red Sea, the promulgation of the law on Mount Sinai, the tabernacle, the ark, the two tables of stone, or to the encampments and wanderings of Israel in the deserts of Arabia, although these desert wildernesses of Arabia could not have been far distant from the abodes of Job and his three friends, and probably were oft frequented by the patriarch. Hence these events were posterior to the patriarchal æra of Job. This Poem contains not the most distant allusion to the call of Abraham, the Abrahamic covenant, or the conflagration of the cities of the plain. Hence we conclude that the æra of Abraham and Lot was posterior to the patriarchal æra of Job.

Job lived 140 years after his restoration to prosperity.

Previously to his sufferings and buffeting by Satan he had ten children, who had all attained to maturity of age. Hence, in all probability, his longevity must have nearly (possibly quite) amounted to 300 years. Before the Deluge, human longevity was little short of 1000 years. After the Deluge, the age of man was on a declining scale, from 600 years, the age of Shem, to the present contracted span of human life as described in Psalm xc.[1] Now as Peleg and Reu each

---

[1] See the author's version of Psalm xc. in his *Psalterium Messianicum Davidis Regis et Prophetæ*, wherein it is shown that threescore years and ten were the predicted measure of the life of David, and that EIGHTY YEARS AND UPWARDS (not seventy years) constitute the present span of human longevity, as defined by the royal Psalmist.

died at the age of 239, and Serug at the age of 230, we may infer that Job, Eliphaz, Bildad, and Zophar, if not anterior to, were coetaneous with, these three patriarchs, and also with Shem, Arphaxad, Salah, and Eber. This calculation of the ante-Abrahamic age, when Job lived, accords with the statement of Abulfaragius,[1] that Job's temptation by Satan occurred in the twenty-fifth year of the life of Nahor. Now Nahor, the son of Serug, was born Anno Mundi 1849, and Job's temptation is said by Abulfaragius to have occurred twenty-five years after, that is, Anno Mundi 1874. Hales,[2] in his *Sacred Chronology*, from astronomical observations, assigns the time of Job's trial to "the year B.C. 2337 ; or 818 years after the Deluge ; 184 years before the birth of Abraham ; 474 years before the settlement of Jacob's family in Egypt ; and 689 years before their EXODE, or their departure from thence. That Job, Eliphaz, Bildad, and Zophar lived in the patriarchal age before the days of Abraham, has the express sanction of Bishop Lowth :—" De ætate Jobi ipsius, quamquam accurate definiri non potest, non tamen video, cur multum dubitemus. Mose antiquiorem fuisse, ac ÆQUALEM ETIAM PATRIARCHIS, ipsius longa ætas indicat."
—*Bishop Lowth.*

THE AUTHOR AND DICTION OF THE BOOK OF JOB.

The authorship of the Book of Job has exercised many pens, and filled many volumes, and yet remains in its pristine obscurity and doubt. No man knoweth who committed to writing this sacred Poem, or how or when it was incorporated into the Hagiographa of the Hebrew Scriptures. Revelation alone could disclose the mystery, and revelation is silent. Two facts, however, are self-evident :—I. The whole Book of Job, as we now possess it, must have proceeded from one inspired writer, because the speeches, separate from the Prologue

---

[1] The statement of Abulfaragius is : "In the twenty-fifth year of the life of Nahor occurred the temptation of Job the Just, according to the opinion of Arudh the Canaanite."

[2] See Hales's "Time of Job," in his second volume, page 57. The above computation of Hales essentially differs from the commonly received chronology. The chronology of Hales is based on the chronology of the Septuagint.

and Epilogue, reveal neither their origin, cause, nor effect, and would so far be unintelligible; and because the Prologue and Epilogue, separate from the body of the Poem, would be a disjointed historical fragment. The argument of Bishop Lowth to establish this fact is unanswerable, and incontrovertible:—"Esse Prologum et Epilogum quodammodo extra ipsum opus, et argumentum Poematis explicare, manifestum est: sed EJUSDEM ESSE CUM POEMATE ET ÆTATIS ET AUCTORIS, ex eo patet, quod ad nodi solutionem, quae in ipso Poemate non datur, sint necessarii." II. Many writers attribute the authorship to Job himself. This is an impossibility. The writer narrates the death of Job. No man can be the historian of his own decease. The knowledge of the writer of the Poem of Job is a matter of very minor importance. It is sufficient for us to be assured, that the author, whoever the author may have been, wrote as he was moved by the Holy Ghost, and that the Book of Job is an integral portion of Jehovah's revelation to man, whereby all will be judged at the last Great Day. The covenant-God of the spiritual Israel, out of His abundant love and mercy to His Church, would have revealed the author of the Book of Job, had He adjudged such revelation essential to man's edification. The Divine reticence should impress on our hearts, "Where ignorance is bliss, 'tis folly to be wise."

The proximity of the residence of Job, Eliphaz, Bildad, and Zophar to the mountain-peaks of Hermon, Sunnin, and Mukhmal indicates, why the diction of this Poem is the pure Hebrew of the ante-Abrahamic age—Hebrew the language of the whole of Canaan—Hebrew the language yet extant in Phœnician characters on the ancient coins and sculptured marbles and stones of Tyrian colonies, extending from Aradus in the extreme north of Phœnicia to Marseilles in France. The few Arabic words, proverbs, idioms, and significations occurring in the Book of Job are Hebrew archaisms still current in Arabic, the sister dialect of Hebrew, but obsolete and no longer found in the fragmentary remains of the Hebrew language now extant. The Book of Job, unique in antiquity and sublimity, is written in pure archaic Hebrew, a noble specimen of the ancient Hebrew language, as it was spoken and written more than 4000 years ago.

The most interesting question respecting the diction is, whether the speeches were originally delivered as they have been recorded and handed down in the Hebrew Scriptures, or whether the writer, under the afflatus of the Spirit, has expressed in poetry what was first of all spoken in prose; that is, whether the author has expressed in his own language the sentiments of the respective speakers, whilst preserved from all possibility of error by the infallible guidance of inspiration. The extempore delivery in rhyme of such sententious, elaborate, argumentative, and sublime poetic speeches would seem an impossibility. But their delivery in Hebrew parallelisms is accordant with oriental usage, and their extempore delivery in parallelisms may even be deemed possible, if not probable. That the speeches were delivered as we now have them is the cherished opinion of the author, which opinion he presents with diffidence and deference to the consideration of the reader. Furthermore, the author submits that there is no notation of time in the Book of Job from the beginning of the third chapter to the end of the thirty-first. Hence the hypothesis, that the speeches of Job, Eliphaz, Bildad, and Zophar were not uttered in immediate succession one after another, without any intervention of time, but that some interval may have elapsed between each speech, and the reply thereto, contradicts neither the letter nor the spirit of the Poem. According to this hypothesis, the speeches may all have been premeditated and precomposed before their delivery, and consequently may all have been expressed in parallelistic Hebrew poetry, as they are handed down in the Divinely-inspired original.

As, in the author's judgment, the temptation of Job preceded in order of time the facts recorded of Abraham, and as the speeches, if not the facts connected with the temptation, must have been committed to writing contemporaneously with the temptation itself, or immediately afterwards, it would seem at least probable, if not certain, that the Poem of Job is more ancient than all the other Books comprising the Old Testament, and is the oldest Book now extant in the world, having existed more than 3700 years anterior to the present æra, according to our Bible chronology, and above 4100 years according to the interpretation of the Assyrian tablets by Mr. Smith, who identifies Kudur-Mabuk, otherwise called Kuder-laganaru, king of

Elam, with the Chedorlaomer of our Bible. The Poem of Job is quoted, or alluded to, by writers of the Old as well as of the New Testament, but not one of these inspired writers is ever quoted in this Poem, because of the pre-existence of Job before any other Book of the Bible was revealed to man by the inspiration of the Spirit.

The Prologue and Epilogue are manifestly less sublimely poetic than the Poem itself, but are easily divisible into parallel lines, and are therefore expressed in parallelisms, but are not divided, like the Poem itself, into stanzas of two and three lines. The diction of this Poem is extraordinarily interrogative. What poem is there in any language containing so many questions in proportion to its length? Not only are the interrogative particles of frequent occurrence in the original, but in many passages they are understood, and must be expressed in any translation to render it intelligible and coherent.

THE TEACHING OF THE BOOK OF JOB.

Voluminous have been the treatises written on the design, purport, and teaching of the Book of Job. Why it should be deemed more essential to ascertain these particulars respecting the Book of Job than respecting any other Book of the inspired Canon, the author cannot divine. This Poem seems to teach prominently and pre-eminently that Job's afflictions were mercifully designed to inculcate on this Arabian Sheik, "sincere and upright, who feared God, and eschewed evil, great beyond all the sons of the East," the duty of implicit submission to the will of Jehovah, the Creator, Preserver, and Administrator of the universe, the Arbiter of human affairs, the Governor of all things in heaven and on earth, according to the sovereignty of His divine counsels. This Poem magnifies the sovereignty of Jehovah in grace and providence, that "He hath mercy on whom He will have mercy, and whom He will He hardeneth" (*Romans* ix. 18), and that He doeth all things well in time and in eternity. And it affirms that passive obedience, non-resistance, and willing submission to this Divine will, is man's bounden duty, consummate wisdom, and bliss supreme.

This Poem teacheth that Job's afflictions, visited upon him by

Satanic agency, were graciously overruled to humble his soul in the dust by conviction of sin, original and actual—sin against God and man—sin of thought, word, and deed—sin committed in ignorance—sin forgotten, but by this sanctified affliction brought to remembrance, unto his humiliation and edification.

This Poem teacheth, that it was God's gracious design to reveal to Job more fully and distinctly the promised Seed of the woman, who was to bruise the serpent's head, the predicted Messiah, the one Mediator between God and man, the Redeemer, Justifier, Saviour, Law-fulfiller, and Ransom of all who trust in Him, the Supreme Judge of quick and dead, of whom Job had prophesied, and of whom by an assured faith he testifies, that this Saviour was HIS Saviour, HIS hope, and joy, and crown of rejoicing,

> "Whom I shall see MINE OWN,
> And mine eyes shall behold Him, YEA NOT ESTRANGED,
> Though my reins shall have been consumed within me."

One design of this sublime Poem is to exhibit as a pattern for our imitation Job's patient continuance in well-doing, the perpetuity of his faith, the indefectibility of his grace, his final perseverance in walking with God, when persecuted by Satan, stripped of family, friends, and possessions, and deprived of the sensible light of God's countenance, which had formerly irradiated and gladdened his soul. Job, notwithstanding intemperate language, hasty tempers, and passionate reclamations, was upheld by Power divine, and was kept by the power of God through faith unto salvation. In Job was exemplified the promise, that "neither death nor life, nor angels, nor principalities, nor powers, nor things present, nor things to come, nor height, nor depth, nor any other creature, shall be able to separate the children of God from the love of God, which is in Christ Jesus the Lord" (*Romans* viii. 38, 39). Final perseverance is the characteristic, and also the inseparable concomitant, of saving faith. Men cannot be in Christ to-day, and lifting up their eyes in torment to-morrow. They who are saved are saved with an everlasting salvation—saved in time, and saved through the countless ages of eternity. "I am Jehovah, I change not" (*Malachi* iii. 6). Multitudes of professors have fallen finally, but never one possessor.

> "The work which God's goodness began,
> The arm of His strength will complete;
> His promise is Yea and Amen,
> And never was forfeited yet.
> Things future, nor things that are now,
> Not all things below nor above,
> Can make Him His purpose forego,
> Or sever my soul from His love.
>
> My name from the palms of His hands
> Eternity will not erase;
> Imprest on His heart it remains,
> In marks of indelible grace:
> Yes, I to the end shall endure,
> As sure as the earnest is given;
> More happy, but not more secure,
> The glorified spirits in heaven."—*Toplady.*

Job more clearly apprehended, more highly appreciated and more fully realized, the doctrines of grace, than many religionists in these last days of Laodicean lukewarmness—these last days perilous to the souls of men.

As Satan's temptations were overruled to the greater sanctification of Job, and to his more intimate communion and walk with God, so the Book of Job exhibits for our imitation the patient forbearance of the agonized Patriarch under the caustic aspersions and unfounded accusations of his three mistaken friends. Never once did Job interrupt their speeches, nor interpose his voice, before they had exhausted their arguments, and had uttered all their embittered sayings. Nor did Eliphaz, Shuah, and Zophar ever once interrupt Job. Contrast this patient forbearance with the clamorous vociferations, the savage obstructing yells, the reckless demolition of property, and the personal injuries not infrequently witnessed during elections of members of Parliament. The patience and forbearance of these patriarchal sons of the East should shame the peccant disciples of the Prince of Peace, and should teach them that "the wrath of man worketh not the righteousness of God" (*James* i. 20).

Satan's assault upon Job should, moreover, remind every reader, that by mysterious permission the fallen Spirit is yet the God of this world, and the Prince of the power of the air, ever "roaming to and fro IN THE EARTH, and walking up and down in it." Satan yet exercises dominant power over the unregenerate, instilling into their mind strong delusion, that they should believe a lie. The same warfare with which Satan persecuted Job, he now wageth, as far as permitted, against the children of God. Hence results the duty of a DAILY oblation of the petition, which Christ Himself hath commanded: "Deliver us from the Evil One." As the demoniacal possession of the bodies of men characterized the Incarnation, so Satan's possession of the souls of men is one of the remarkable signs of the present day, one of the striking features of the termination of "the times of the Gentiles," one of the prominent characteristics of Laodicean lukewarmness, the immediate predicted prelude to the close of the present dispensation: "Therefore be ye also ready, for in such an hour as ye think not, the Son of Man cometh" (*Matthew* xxiv. 44).

If the judgment of Chrysostom[1] and Cæsarius be pronounced correct, that THE SONS OF GOD in Scripture never signify angels, but always the regenerate, the justified, the sanctified, those who are the children of God by adoption and grace, those who are the children of God by possession or profession—if the monstrous figment, that the intermarriages of the angelic and Adamic races are recorded in Genesis vi., be worthily consigned to the grave of all the Capulets, it will follow that this Poem advocates the universal and perpetual observance of an hebdomadal Sabbath. When in Paradise God blessed and sanctified the seventh day, He blessed and sanctified it to Adam as the federal head of the whole human race, and therefore through Adam enjoined its sanctification on all his posterity of every age and every clime. The institution of the Sabbath in Paradise was after the six days' work of creation. The renewed command on Mount Sinai was after six days of consecutive secular labour. No particular

---

[1] Δειξατωσαν, που αγγελοι υιοι Θεου προσηγορευθησαν. Αλλ' ουκ αν εχοιεν ουδαμου δειξαι· ανθρωποι μεν γαρ εκληθησαν υιοι Θεου, αγγελοι δε ουδαμως.—Chrysostomi, *Homil.* xxii. *in Genesin.* Ουδεπω αγγελοι υιοι Θεου προςαγορευονται.—*Cæsarii*, Dial. I. Interrog. xlviii.

day is specified in either case, because the command is of universal obligation, and it is impossible that the whole human race can sanctify one and the same day, it being day in one part of the globe, when it is night in another part.

If these premises be admitted, this Poem inculcates the sanctification of an hebdomadal Sabbath, and exhibits for our imitation the example of Job and his neighbours of North-Western Arabia attending public worship as an essential branch of Sabbath sanctification. The Sabbath is not only an enjoined duty, but a blessing and privilege to nations, families, individuals, yea to the whole human race, who observe it. The Sabbath is the Lord's Day. Christ is the Lord of the Sabbath. Where the Sabbath is habitually desecrated, there heartfelt religion must decrease. Experience will ever prove, that the religious observance of the Sabbath and self-dedication to God on His day, have the promise of the life that now is, and of that which is to come.

The creed of Job, enunciated in this archaic Poem for our admonition and instruction on whom the ends of the world are come, was "Jehovah thy Gods is one Jehovah" (*Deuteronomy* vi. 4). Job worshipped the triune God, afterwards more fully revealed to man in the volume of Revelation, the holy, holy, holy Lord God of hosts, with whose glory heaven and earth are replete. Job worshipped the Holy Ones, coequal, coeternal, and coessential (v. 1). Job knew the true God experimentally as his covenant-God in and through the promised predicted Redeemer. Job, moreover, anticipated a blissful resurrection, when, in perfect sanctification and plenitude of glory, he should see God face to face, and be ever with God, and with the people of God, through the countless ages of eternity. He neither prayed to the dead, nor for the dead. He knew no Mediator with God but Messiah his Redeemer, Resurrection, and Life. He knew not the Moslem-God, "who neither begets nor is begotten." He knew not the God of Socinus, the unhallowed fiction of a depraved imagination.

The purport of the Book of Job is the same as the purport of all the other books of the Old and New Testament, "to humble the sinner, exalt the Saviour, and promote holiness of life."

PLAN OF THE WORK.

The translation is made from the received Hebrew text of Vander Hooght, 1705 (omitting all reference to the Masoretic punctuation, man's addition to God's word written), unless where a different reading is proposed in the Critical Appendix. The design of the Translation and of the Notes appended thereto is to render the Book of Job intelligible, attractive, and edifying to the English reader. The deviations of this translation from the Authorized English Bible (which is grounded chiefly on the Ancient Versions), are justifiable to obviate obscurity, rectify misinterpretations, and exhibit more fully the poetic beauties of the sublime original. Bishop Wordsworth has correctly remarked, that "there is no book of the Old Testament, on the language of which so much light has been shown by the philology of the last and present centuries, as the Book of Job. The Ancient Versions of this Book, especially the Septuagint, are not satisfactory." Hemistichs equivalent to more than 100 verses of the Hebrew original are wanting in this exceptional portion[1] of the venerable LXX. Version, as the LXX. Version of the Book of Job is said to have existed before the days of Origen. What reliance can be placed on this exceptional portion of the LXX. Version, presenting so many lacunæ, besides several interpolations?

Notes are appended to explain and illustrate Oriental idioms and allusions, to elucidate obscurities, and to vindicate what is novel in the translation or interpretation. Of many of the animals,[2] constel-

---

[1] The reader will find, in the various readings under the text in Jahn's edition of the Hebrew Bible, a specific statement of the hemistichs and entire verses wanting in the LXX. Version of the Book of Job BEFORE THE TIME OF ORIGEN. The same are marked * in the different readings of the *Codex Alexandrinus* in Holmes' and Parson's Septuagint. "* Hoc signum Origenes præmisit vocibus iis, quas ex Versionibus aliorum interpretum Græcorum in textum Septuaginta-viralem induxerat."

"The translation of Job exhibits very obvious traces of carelessness and incompetency on the part of the Septuagint translators."—Fairbairn's *Bible Dictionary.*

"It is well known that the Septuagint contains innumerable gross errors and interpolations."—*The Two Babylons*, by Rev. A. Hislop.

[2] In the enumeration of animals cited in manifestation of the omnipotence of Jehovah

lations, metals, and idiomatic phrases occurring in this Poem, explanation will be found in these Notes. The Critical Appendix exhibits some rays of the light which has been shed on this most ancient Poem by reference to the Arabic language.

The Book of Job contains many parabolic sententious sayings current in the patriarchal ages before the time of Abraham. The general meaning of these parables is self-evident from the context. The special circumstances however whence they originated, their local allusions, and the definite signification of some terms employed (especially where there occurs an amphibology or play upon words having a twofold meaning), are all lost to us in the hoar of antiquity. The centuries of Arabian adages and proverbs published by Golius, and the more extended collection of Arabian proverbs by Meidanius, reflect no light on these difficulties. Nor should this be matter of surprise. Of the remains of the Arabic language which have come down to us, very few fragments indeed are earlier than the Hegira of Mohammed, A.D. 622, and therefore their antiquity is less than 1300 years, whereas the proverbs embodied in the Book of Job were current certainly more than 3700 years, and, as the Author believes, more than 4000 years ago. These patriarchal proverbs and sententious sayings are printed in black-letter.

The Author has amassed, with much difficulty and research, very many works illustrative of the Book of Job, and from them has derived light, knowledge, and information. These he has diligently consulted, particularly on controverted subjects and difficult texts. But the translation and interpretation of the Book of Job proposed in this volume are grounded on the original Hebrew of the Book itself. The

---

as Creator, Preserver, and Administrator of the universe, no mention occurs of the CAMEL—the ship of the desert—the most valuable of all the beasts of burden in the East—without whose valuable aid the trackless wildernesses of Arabia could not be traversed—of which, before his temptation, Job possessed 3000, and after his restoration to prosperity 6000. The lion, the raven, the rock-goat, the wild ass, the wild ox, the ostrich, the war-horse, the hawk, the eagle, the crocodile are named, but not the abstemious, sure-footed, though gaunt unsightly camel. To what cause can be assigned this preterition of the camel, whose special adaptation to the arid deserts of the East is so signal a manifestation of the creative power, beneficence, and goodness of Jehovah, and of His merciful supervision of the universe?

earnest endeavour of the author has been to express freely and fully, without reservation or preterition, what, in his apprehension, God has taught man in the Hebrew poem of Job. To two writers he is more especially indebted, John Mason Good, M.D., and Albert Schultens. From the former he has borrowed some expositions of difficult passages, and several felicitous expressions of poetic diction. To the latter he is indelibly indebted, in common with all who have subsequently written on the Book of Job. Every line of his Latin Version has been carefully scanned and compared with the Hebrew text. For patient labour in the collection and classification of olden interpretations, for minute and extensive Oriental research, for successful elucidation of obscure passages, for literary honesty and genuine humility in confessing his doubts and misgivings of his own interpretations of this most ancient and sublime Poem, Albert Schultens shines without a rival. His two quarto volumes, published 1737, shed a halo of light on the difficulties and obscurities of the Book of Job, and may be considered the first bright rays of that philology which has continued progressively to illustrate this unique remnant of Arabian literature.

For a most able delineation of patriarchal religion, extending from Creation to the æra of Job, the reader is referred to Biddulph's *Theology of the Early Patriarchs, illustrated by an appeal to subsequent parts of the Holy Scriptures.*

May Jehovah, the covenant God of the ancient patriarch of Arabia, pardon the errors, shortcomings, and defects of the Author! May He bless this volume, as far as it is accordant with His revealed will, to the elucidation of His word, the vindication of His truth, the rectification of error, and the manifestation of Christ to the soul of every reader! May He sanctify Job's faith and patient continuance in well-doing to all the members of the mystical body of Christ, that the children of God, of every clime and every denomination, may be fortified and prepared against that apostasy from the pure Gospel, against that crash of nations, and against those final judgments on a benighted world, which are the premonitory signs and predicted harbingers of the Second Advent of Christ in glory!

RYDE, *June* 1869.

CORRIGENDA.

Page 7. Chapter II. Verse 10.
 Add, In all this did not Job sin with his lips.
Page 8. Chapter II. Verse 11.
 For, the evil, *read*, this evil.
Page 24. Chapter IX. Verse 9.
 For, Cimah, *read*, And Cimah.
Page 26. Chapter IX. Verse 32.
 For, and that, *read*, That.
Page 31. Line 37.
 For, summer disappear in the winter, *read*, winter disappear in the summer.
Page 54. Chapter XXI. Verse 29.
 For, thou canst, *read*, you can.
 For, thou couldest, *read*, you could.
Page 104. Lines 1 and 2.
 For, Leviathan, *read*, Behemoth.
Page 104. Line 44.
 For, condoes, *read*, coudees.

THE BOOK OF JOB.

THE PROLOGUE.

CHAPTER I.—VERSES 1-5.

Job's place of residence, his piety, his family, his possessions, his religious supervision of his children, and his anxious solicitude for their spiritual welfare.

1 THERE was a man in the land of Uz, whose name was Job,
  And this man was sincere and upright,
  And he feared God, and eschewed evil.
2 And unto him were born seven sons and three daughters,
3 And his stock of cattle was seven thousand sheep,
  And three thousand camels,
  And five hundred yoke of oxen,
  And five hundred she-asses,
  And his husbandry-servants were very numerous,
  So that this man was great beyond all the sons of the East.

4 And his sons were wont to make a feast
  In the house of each one on his birthday,
  When they sent and invited their three sisters
  To eat and to drink together with them.
5 And it came to pass when the feast-days had gone round,
  That Job sent and sanctified them,
  And rose up early in the morning, and offered burnt-offerings
  According to the number of them all.
  For Job said:
  " Peradventure my sons may have sinned,
  And have not blessed God in their hearts."
  Thus did Job continually.

CHAP. I. VER. 1.—*Job.*—Proper names occurring in the Hebrew Scriptures are significant, and the signification of most Hebrew proper names is known. The name JOB is the pahul or past participle of a Hebrew verb signifying TO BE AN ENEMY TO, TO PERSECUTE. " Hence JOB in Hebrew signifies THE PERSECUTED ONE."—*Parkhurst's Hebrew Lexicon.* The identity of the signification of the Hebrew verb whence JOB is derived, with the signification of the Hebrew verb from which SATAN is derived, seems at least obliquely to imply that Satan was the instigator and instrument of Job's persecution. " Nomen proprie valet HOSTILITER TRACTATUM. Hominem intellige (a Satana) hostiliter tractatum, qualem fuisset Jobum, integrum quod de eo agit carmen didacticum docet."—*Gesenii Thesaurus Theologicus.*

VER. 1. *Sincere*—PERFECT, the rendering of our authorized version, and of very many translations of the Book of Job, is liable to mislead the English reader, and to establish doctrinal error. Sinless perfection is not the doctrine of the Bible, nor is it the experience of God's children. There is no man alive that sinneth not. In our flesh dwelleth no good thing. In many things we offend all. Job was not perfect either in the sight of God or man, according to his own confession :

" Should I justify myself, my own mouth would condemn me.
I know not perfection ;
If I did, I myself should disown my own being."—ix. 20, 21.
" Behold, I am vile ; what shall I answer Thee ?"—xl. 4.

SINCERITY, etymologically deriving its signification from pure honey unmixed with wax, seems fully to express in English the meaning of the inspired original. The character of Job corresponded with that of the Philippian converts, for whom St. Paul prayed that " they might be sincere and without offence, filled with the fruit of righteousness unto the glory and praise of God."—*Philippians* i. 10, 11. " This word seems to be synonymous with the Greek τέλειος, 1 Cor. ii. 6 ; xiv. 20, etc., and to signify COMPLETE in every requisite of true religion, thoroughly furnished unto all good works, rather than PERFECT in the abstract."—*Lee.* " Job, having a respect to all God's commandments, aiming at perfection, was really as good as he seemed to be, and did not dissemble in his profession of piety. His heart was sound, and his eye single. SINCERITY IS GOSPEL PERFECTION. I know no religion without it."—*Henry.*

VER. 1. *Feared.*—' The term FEAR, which, among the writers of the Old Testament, so frequently expresses the religious principle generally, does not necessarily denote that apprehension of danger or of wrath, which the Apostle tells us ' perfect love casteth out,' but only that feeling of awe and reverence, which cannot be separated from the creature's admiration of the Great God—the fear and trembling with which His worship and service must be attended by pious minds, though all His goodness be made to pass before them, and those attributes of Deity, which might well create alarm, be screened by revealed and pledged mercies."—*Fry.*

VER. 4. *Feast.*—The family banquet given by each of Job's sons on his birthday was not in itself sinful, but is rather to be commended. Solomon must have been conversant with the Book of Job, and with this recorded practice of the sons of Job, the oriental Sheikh, " great beyond all the sons of the East." His inspired language is expressive of commendation, not of censure :

" Behold, I have considered that it is good, that it is comely,
That a man should eat and drink and experience delight in all his labour,
Wherein he laboureth under the sun,
During the number of the days of his life which God hath assigned him,
Truly this is his allotted portion.
Yea, to every man to whom God hath given riches and wealth,
And hath enabled him to eat thereof,
And to sustain his allotted portion, and to rejoice in his labour,
This is the very gift of God."—*Ecclesiastes,* v. 18, 19.

VER. 4. *House.*—It is self-evident from Job xxi. 28,
" For ye say, Where is the HOUSE of the noble ?
Where is the TENT, the habitation, of the wicked ?"

where the HOUSE and the TENT are distinguished from each other, that even in the early days of Job many Orientals dwelt in substantial houses, and not in mere tents, and that Job and his sons dwelt in houses built, and not in tents pitched. As the building of cities and houses began in the days of Cain, so the same erections seem to have been practised soon after the deluge. This proves that Job and his family were stationary residents, and not migratory nomads.

VER. 5. *Burnt-offerings.*—Before the institution of the Mosaic law on Mount Sinai, every father of a family was a priest to his own household, and for himself and for them offered sacrifices for sin. Wherever Abraham pitched his tent, he erected a sacrificial altar. These sacrifices were typical of the vicarious death and passion of the predicted Messiah, the Lamb slain in the counsels of Jehovah before the foundation of the world. "The custom of offering sacrifice was of Divine institution, was in use from the fall of man, and was by tradition handed down from one to another, and so Job had it. Job, by faith in Christ, offered up those burnt-offerings for his sons, and one for each of them, thereby signifying that every one stood in need of the whole sacrifice of Christ for the atonement of sin, as every sinner does."—*Dr. Gill.*

VER. 5. *Have not blessed God in their hearts.*—Job does not suspect his sons of any overt acts of irreligion or immorality, but rather of sins of omission, being fearful that in their festive hours they may not have had God in all their thoughts, and may have omitted to praise Him, the author and source of all their mercies. The good old practice of our feasts being sanctified by the Word of God and prayer is too often neglected in these perilous times of the last days, in these last days of Laodicean lukewarmness and apostasy. The above is substantially the version of Mason Good. The Coptic version is very similar: "Lest my sons should have thought evil in their hearts towards God."

CHAPTER I.—VERSES 6-22.

Observance of the hebdomadal Sabbath by the inhabitants of North Arabia, the first command which God gave to His creature man, which command was continuously and universally observed by the faithful from the creation of Adam and Eve unto the days of Job. This presence at public worship was an essential branch of their Sabbath-sanctification. Jehovah interrogates Satan (present, though invisible to mortal eyes, among the worshippers of the one living and true God), and grants to him mysterious permission to strip Job of his earthly possessions, his servants, and his children. Satan exercised the power, which, by calumniation of Job, he had obtained. Job, despoiled by Satan of his wealth and children, with believing submission to the Divine will, praiseth God for what He had providentially given, and for what He had providentially taken away.

6 AND the day was, when the sons of God came
 To present themselves before Jehovah,
 And Satan came in also among them.
7 And Jehovah said unto Satan: "From whence comest thou?"
 And Satan answered Jehovah, and said:
 "From roaming to and fro in the earth, and from walking up and
  down in it."
8 And Jehovah said unto Satan:
 "Hast thou well considered my servant Job,
 That there is none like unto him upon the earth,
 A man sincere and upright,
 Fearing God and eschewing evil?"
9 Then Satan answered Jehovah, and said:
 "Does Job fear God for nought?
10 Hast Thou not made a fence about him,

And about his family, and about all that pertains to him on every
    side?
The work of his hands Thou hast blessed,
And his stock of cattle hath overspread the land.
11 But indeed put forth now Thine hand,
And smite all that pertains to him.
Whilst Thou smitest him not, he will bless Thee to Thy face."
12 And Jehovah said unto Satan:
" Behold, all that pertains to him is in thy power,
Only against himself stretch not forth thine hand."
And Satan went forth from the presence of Jehovah.

13 And the day was, when his sons and his daughters
Were eating and drinking wine
In their eldest brother's house.
14 And a messenger came unto Job, and said:
" The oxen were ploughing
And the she-asses were grazing, both as they were wont,
15 And the Sabæans fell upon them and seized them,
And have slain the servants with the edge of the sword,
And I only have escaped, myself alone, to tell thee."
16 While this one was yet speaking, another also came in, and said:
" The fire of God hath fallen from heaven,
And hath burned the sheep, and the servants, and consumed them,
And I only have escaped, myself alone, to tell thee."
17 While this one was yet speaking, another also came in, and said:
" The Chaldæans formed three bands,
And rushed upon the camels, and carried them away,
And have slain the servants with the edge of the sword,
And I only have escaped, myself alone, to tell thee."
18 While this one was yet speaking, another also came in, and said:
" Thy sons and thy daughters were eating and drinking wine
In their eldest brother's house,
19 And lo! a great wind came from across the desert,
And struck the four corners of the house,
And it fell upon the young people, and they are dead,
And I only have escaped, myself alone, to tell thee."
20 Then Job arose, and rent his mantle,

And shaved his head,
21 And fell on the ground, and worshipped, and said:
"Naked came I forth from my mother's womb,
And naked shall I return thither;
Jehovah hath given, and Jehovah hath taken away,
Blessed be the name of Jehovah."
22 In all this Job sinned not,
And imputed not default to God.

CHAP. I. VER. 6. *And the day was when the sons of God came.*—The interpretation of this verse, that the SONS OF GOD signify ANGELS, and that THE PLACE where the Sons of God presented themselves before Jehovah signifies HEAVEN, rests on no warrant of Scripture, and is *toto cœlo* inadmissible. The Hebrew phrase, THE SONS OF GOD, occurs in Genesis vi. 2, 4; Job i. 6, ii. 1, and xxxviii. 7. There is a somewhat similar phrase in Hosea i. 10. This interpretation in Genesis of THE SONS OF GOD, that they signify ANGELS, supposes intermarriages between the Angelic and Adamic races, and the birth of a progeny gigantic in stature and wickedness: a suppositious and incredible monstrosity. The absurdity of this misapprehension of antediluvian history, by whatever great names it may have been advocated, is its own confutation. This interpretation of Job i. 6 and ii. 1 supposes, that there is a fixed time when God periodically meets the Angelic host in heaven,—an assertion not corroborated by Scripture; and it inferentially asserts that Satan, expelled from heaven, has the power to re-enter heaven when and where he pleases, and to intermingle with the elect Angels ever singing: "Holy, holy, holy, Lord of hosts, the whole earth is full of Thy glory." THE SONS OF GOD in Genesis are the descendants of Seth, or antediluvian believers in general. Intermarriages between the Church and the world, between those who feared Jehovah and those who feared Him not, were productive of those sins which caused the Deluge. THE SONS OF GOD and THE MORNING STARS (*Job* xxxviii. 7) are the family of Noah, the second universal father of the human race, who "sang together" in praise to God, and "shouted for joy" when the punishment of the Deluge ceased, and the earth was again fitted for man's habitation. The day on which the SONS OF GOD of North Arabia presented themselves before Jehovah was the Sabbath-day, which God had blessed and sanctified, and which they observed by assembling together for public worship. The presence of Satan, visible to God alone, is no more than what the evil Spirit now practises to distract the thoughts of saints engaged in Sabbatic worship, and to eradicate, if possible, the seed of the Gospel sown, that it take not root downwards and bear not fruit upwards. Chrysostom and Cæsarius affirm that the phrase, THE SONS OF GOD, NEVER signifies ANGELS.—See *Suiceri Thesaurus*, tom. i. p. 38. In Hebrews i. 5 we read: "Unto which of the Angels said He AT ANY TIME: Thou art My Son, this day have I begotten thee?" Luther declares "that Moses calleth the SONS OF GOD men who had an interest in the promise of the Blessed Seed, who call God Father, and whom God on His part calleth Sons." "SONS OF GOD, in the language of the Old and New Testaments, are those who are born to God, of the Church, in distinction from unbelievers."—*Julius Bate*. "SONS OF GOD are men begotten again or formed by His Word and Spirit, and resembling their heavenly Father in their dispositions and actions (Gen. vi. 2, 4), where the believing line of Seth are distinguished by this title from the daughters of men, *i.e.*, women of the apostate race of Cain."—*Parkhurst*. The Coptic version renders the end of this verse: "the Devil came also with them, and STOOD UPON THE EARTH, and passed over it." "Est-il historiquement vrai, que Dieu tienne dans le ciel, avec ses anges, une cour de justice; que Satan ait la liberté de s'y présenter et de parler familièrement avec Dieu?"—*Bridel*. We may therefore safely conclude that THE SONS OF GOD named in this verse are WORSHIPPERS from North Arabia, and that the day on which they were assembled was THE SABBATH-DAY, which God had commanded to be kept holy. Whether the interlocution between Jehovah and Satan occurred in heaven or upon earth, at the suppositious periodical assembly of the pan-angelic synod, or on the Sabbath-day, the mystery must be one and the same, above the ken of human intelligence, never to be comprehended, until delivered from the burden of the flesh man shall see as he is seen, and know as he is known.

VER. 6. *Satan.*—Schultens considers the evil Spirit to be so named, because he is the malign adversary of God and man. "Ab obstinatissimâ adversatione dictus fuerit Satanas. Cernis e vestigio intensissimum, obstinatissimum et impudentissimum studium adversandi. Satanas, præter notissimum usum, significat omnem pervicaciter rebellem, qua hominem, qua genium, qua bestiam."

VER. 8. *My servant.*—The expression MY SERVANT is of frequent occurrence in Scripture, but is never predicated by the Holy Spirit of any but of Christ the Head and the members of His mystical body. It is predicated of Christ, Abraham, Jacob, Moses, Caleb, Isaiah, Eliakim, Zerubbabel, Nebuchadnezzar, as well as of Job. Hence we may infer that Nebuchadnezzar, after his recovery from his judicially inflicted insanity, was possessed of Divine justifying faith, that he died the believing head of an idolatrous empire, and that at death he entered into that rest which remaineth to the people of God. "Thou art this head of gold" (*Daniel* ii. 38). Hence it is self-evident, that Job was regenerated, justified, sanctified, and saved, before he was buffeted by Satan, though his faith was weak, and his religious knowledge imperfect, as were the faith and knowledge of the eleven before the day of Pentecost.

VER. 11. *Whilst Thou smitest him not.*—As long as Thou forbearest to smite and afflict Job, so long will Job worship and bless Thee, and no longer. Smite him. His semblance of religion will be dissipated. He will fear Thee no more for ever.

VER. 13. *The day.*—This day, to which the definite article is prefixed in the original Hebrew, is apparently the birthday of the first-begotten of Job's children, which primogeniture gave him the right of a double portion of the paternal inheritance, and precedence over and above his brothers and sisters.

VER. 19. *The young people.*—All the seven sons and three daughters of Job perished together by one Divine visitation. "They died by a wind of the Devil's raising, who is THE PRINCE OF THE POWER OF THE AIR (Eph. ii. 2), but it was looked upon to be an immediate hand of God, and a token of His wrath. So Bildad construed it (viii. 4). Thy children have sinned against Him, and He has cast them away in their transgression. They were taken away, when he had most need of them to comfort him under all his other losses."—*Henry.*

VER. 21. *Return thither.*—"Return to the house of the grave."—*Chaldee Targum.*

VERS. 20, 21.—"Job does not attribute his losses to second causes, to the Sabæans and Chaldæans, to the fire from heaven, and the wind from the desert, but to God, whose sovereign will and overruling hand were in all. These were but the instruments of Satan, and Satan had no power but what was given him from God. Therefore, to the counsel of His will who suffered it Job refers it."—*Dr. Gill.* "The devil hath taken away nothing but by Divine permission. This permission God gave, that man might be proved, that the devil might be conquered. Let not the enemy triumph, as if he had done it. I know from whom he hath received permission. To the devil be attributed the will to hurt, to my Lord the power of probation. I have lost my gold, I have lost my family, I have lost my cattle, I have lost all my possessions, but I have not lost Him, the gracious giver. I have lost what He hath given, I have not lost Him, whose I am. He is my delight. He is my riches. Let Him take away all things. Let Him strip me naked, and reserve Himself for me. What can I want, if I possess God? What can other things profit me, if I possess not God?"—*Augustine.*

VER. 21. Scott thus beautifully paraphrases the two last lines of this verse:—

"The Lord in bounty gave, but gave in trust,
The Lord resumes; resuming, not unjust:
Giving, resuming, He is still the Lord,
Still be the glories of His name adored."

CHAPTER II.—VERSES 1-13.

Another hebdomadal Sabbath observed and sanctified by worshippers of North Arabia. Jehovah a second time interrogates Satan (again invisible to man, and visible to God only), and grants to Satan mysterious permission to smite the bone and flesh of Job with malignant ulceration. Job, thus smitten, reproves his wife for her faithlessness, and bows submissively to the Divine dispensation. Job's three friends, Eliphaz, Bildad, and Zophar, come to condole with him and to console him.

1 And the day was, when the sons of God came
   To present themselves before Jehovah :
   And Satan came in also among them
   To present himself before Jehovah.
2 And Jehovah said unto Satan : " From whence comest thou ?"
   And Satan answered Jehovah, and said :
   " From running to and fro in the earth, and from walking up and
      down in it."
3 And Jehovah said unto Satan :
   " Hast thou well considered my servant Job,
   That there is none like unto him upon the earth,
   A man sincere and upright,
   Fearing God and eschewing evil,
   And still he holdeth fast his integrity,
   Although thou hast excited me against him to destroy him
      without a cause ?"
4 And Satan answered Jehovah, and said :
   " **Skin for Skin,**
   Yea, all that pertains to a man will he give up for his life.
5 But indeed put forth now Thine hand,
   And smite his bone, and his flesh.
   Whilst Thou smitest him not, he will bless Thee to Thy face."
6 And Jehovah said unto Satan :
   " Behold, he is in thy power, only preserve his life."
7 Then Satan went forth from the presence of Jehovah,
   And smote Job with a malignant ulceration
   From the sole of his foot to the crown of his head.
8 And he took him a potsherd to scrape himself therewith,
   And sat down among the ashes.
9 And his wife said unto him :
   " Even yet dost thou hold fast thine integrity,
   Blessing God, and dying ?"
10 But he said unto her :
   " As speaketh one of the wicked women, so thou speakest,
   Truly we receive good from God,
   And shall we not receive evil ?"

11 Now the three friends of Job had heard

Of all the evil which had befallen him,
And they came each one from his place,
Eliphaz the Temanite, and Bildad the Shuhite, and Zophar the
    Naamathite,
For they had appointed to come together,
To condole with him, and to comfort him.

12 And they raised their eyes from afar, and recognised him not,
And they lifted up their voices and wept,
And rent every one his mantle,
And sprinkled dust upon their heads towards heaven.

13 So they sat down with him upon the ground,
Seven days and seven nights,
And none spake a word unto him,
For they saw that the affliction was exceeding great.

CHAP. II. VER. 3. *My servant.*—See Note on i. 8.

VER. 4. *Skin for skin.*—This archaic proverb, spoken by Satan, has its origin in the two-fold sense attributed by the Orientals to the word SKIN, signifying both THE PERSON and THE PROPERTY of an individual. The meaning of this proverbial saying is self-evident, that property will ever be surrendered for the preservation of life. There seems also an allusion to that terrific SKIN DISEASE, the elephantiasis, which Satan purposed to inflict on the patriarch.

VER. 7. *Malignant ulceration.*—"Most probably the ELEPHAS, ELEPHANTIASIS (ἐλέφαντι, as it is immediately translated in one of the versions of the Hexapla), or leprosy of the Arabians, which, by themselves, is denominated judhám, or, as the word is pronounced in India, juzám, though the Indians in vernacular speech call it khorah. This dreadful malady, which Paul of Ægina has accurately characterized as an universal ulcer, was named ELEPHANTIASIS by the Greeks, from its rendering the skin, like that of the elephant's, scabrous and dark-coloured, and furrowed all over with tubercles. It is said to produce generally in the countenance of the affected a grim, distracted, and lion-like set of features, on which account it is also sometimes denominated in the same language LEONTIASIS."—*J. Mason Good, M.D.*

"In Rio de Janeiro, it is too common a spectacle to see, even among Europeans, as well as native whites and blacks, that dreadful disease, the ELEPHANTIASIS, which, destroying the sound texture of the integuments of the human frame, swells, and distorts, and discolours wherever it attacks, enlarging the patient's misshapen limbs to the bulk of those of the huge animal, the resemblance to whom, in that particular, occasioned the appellation this horrid disease has received."—*Macartney's Embassy to China.*

"Le Démon, après avoir obtenu de Dieu ce pouvoir sur Job, lui souffla par le nez une chaleur si pestilente, que la masse de son sang en fut aussi-tôt corrompue, et que tout son corps ne devint qu'un seul ulcère, dont la puanteur faisoit retirer incontinent tous ceux qui l'approchoient, de sorte que l'on fut obligé de le mettre hors la ville où il habitoit, et le placer en un lieu fort écarté."—*D'Herbelot, Bibliothèque Orientale.*

"ELEPHANTIASIS rend la peau gonflée, rude et inégale, couverte d'écailles avec un grand nombre de sillons et de crevasses, comme celle des éléphants. Les principaux caractères de cette maladie sont la rondeur des yeux et des oreilles, la dépilation, l'élévation de la peau des sourcils, celle de la lèvre supérieure qui laisse les gencives et les dents à nu, la dilatation et la distorsion des narines en dehors, la voix rauque, la puanteur de la bouche et de toute la personne, un regard fixe, et qui fait horreur, la difficulté d'avaler, les songes effrayants, l'insomnie, etc. Job n'est pas plutôt lépreux, qu'il se voit abandonné de sa femme et de ses enfants, que l'odeur insupportable qui s'exhale de tout son corps éloigne de sa présence ; il est négligé par ses serviteurs, et insulté par des gens de la lie du peuple."—*Bridel.*

"Fuit autem ELEPHANTIASIS, turpissimus, dolorificus, molestissimus, ac detestabilis morbus, immedicabilis ex veterum sententiâ, ut vitæ pertæsi nil præter mortem sperare aut optare elephantiaci dicantur; deinde etiam impatientes et iracundos reddere, atque pene rabiem aliquam adferre solet omnia desperantibus, ægre omnia ferentibus."—*Michaelis.*

"In ELEPHANTIA totum corpus afficitur ita, ut ossa quoque vitiari dicantur. Summa pars corporis crebras maculas, crebrosque tumores habet, rubor carum paulatim in atrum colorem convertitur. Summa cutis inæqualiter crassa, tenuis, dura, mollisque, quasi squamis quibusdam exasperatur; corpus emacrescit; os, suræ, pedes intumescunt. Ubi vetus morbus est, digiti in manibus pedibusque sub tumore conduntur. Avicenna dicit, lepram esse quasi cancrum communem toti corpori."—*Celsus.*

VERS. 11-13.—The conduct of Eliphaz, Bildad, and Zophar in coming to condole with and comfort the afflicted patriarch was highly commendable. Their sympathy was genuine and heart-felt. Their patience was exemplary in sitting seven days with Job in silent grief. And though, from erroneous judgment and hasty tempers, they proved in the end miserable comforters, yet their companionship favourably contrasted with the desertion of Job by his relatives and other friends. In them was exemplified the admonition of the wise king of Israel:—

"It is better to go to the house of mourning than to go to the house of feasting,
Because that is the end of all men,
And the living will lay it to his heart.
Better is sorrow than laughter,
Because by dejection of countenance the heart is made better.
The heart of wise men is in the house of mourning,
But the heart of fools is in the house of merriment."—*Ecclesiastes* vii. 2-4.

THE ARGUMENT.

CHAPTER III.—VERSES 1-26.

Job curseth the day of his birth.

1 At length Job opened his mouth,
And cursed the day of his birth.

2 And Job exclaimed and said:

3 Perish the day in which I was born,
And the night which published, A man-child is brought forth.

4 That night, be it darkness!
Let God from on high regard it not!

Yea, let no sunshine irradiate it,
5 Let darkness and the death-shade crush it!

Let the tempest pavilion over it,
The blasts of noon-tide terrify it!

6 That night, let extinction seize it!
Let it not be computed with the days of the year!
Into the number of its months let it not enter.

B

7 Lo! that night! let it be a barren rock!
  Let no peal of gladness resound therein!

8 Let them execrate it, as men promptly curse the day
  Which evoketh the crocodile (from the deep)!

9 Let the stars of its twilight be darkened,
  Let it wait for the light, and have none,
  Yea, let it not behold the glancings of the dawn!

10 Because it closed not the doors of the womb to me,
   Nor hid affliction from mine eyes.

11 Why did I not die (passing) from the womb?
   Why did I not pass from the matrix, and expire?

12 Why did the knees anticipate me?
   And why the breasts, that I should suck?

13 For now should I have lain down and been quiet,
   I should have slept, rest at once would have been mine,

14 With kings and counsellors of the earth,
   Who built habitations for themselves;

15 Or with princes, possessors of gold,
   Who filled their palaces with silver.

16 Or as an unnoticed abortion I had never existed,
   As fœtuses which never saw the light.

17 There the wicked cease from troubling,
   And there the weary are at rest.

18 There the captives rest securely together,
   They hear not the voice of the oppressor.

19 The small and the great are there,
   And the servant is free from his master.

20 Why is life given to the miserable?
   And life to the bitter of soul?

21 (Who long for death, and it is not,
   And dig for it more than for hidden treasures.

22 Who rejoice even to exultation,
   Who exult when they can find the grave.)

23 To the man whose path is broken up,
   And whose futurity God hath overshadowed!

24 For afore my food cometh my sighing,
   And my lamentations burst forth as the billows.

25 Behold, the fear that I feared hath even befallen me,
   And that which I dreaded hath come upon me.

26 I have no peace, yea, I have no quiet,
   Yea, I have no rest, and trouble hath come.

CHAP. III. VER. 8. *Promptly curse the day*—literally, THE PROMPT CURSERS OF THE DAY.—This verse represents the wish of Job, that as men are accustomed to curse the evil day, whereon the crocodile, springing from the deep, destroys men and cattle and pasturage, so they would with equal readiness execrate his natal day, whereon he was born to be despoiled of family and property, to be afflicted with the most grievous disease which flesh is heir to, and to be deprived of the sensible presence of his covenant God through the malignant accusation of the great enemy of Jehovah and of man. The Hebrew word LEVIATHAN, unhappily rendered in our version THEIR MOURNING, is the same noun whereby THE CROCODILE is designated, xli. 1. The description of the crocodile from xl. 15 to xli. 34, under the two names of LEVIATHAN and BEHEMOTH, will explain the terror excited by the desolating ravages of this king over all the sons of pride terrestrial and aquatic. In the days of Job, long before the invention of gunpowder, and the present enormous increase and expansion of the human race, crocodiles were more numerous, had a far wider range, and attained to a much larger size than those seen in the present day.

VER. 14. *Who built habitations for themselves.*—The Authorized Version: "*which built desolate places for themselves,*" though the common interpretation of the Hebrew original, seems inappropriate to the context. The Arabic and other cognate dialects shed no light on the difficulty. But the Coptic noun, answering to the Hebrew, gives us the sense of HABITATIONS, MANSIONS, RESTING-PLACES, DORMITORIES. This term seems comprehensive of habitations for the kings and counsellors whilst living, and of habitations or dormitories for their bodies when dead. The Coptic Lexicon of La Croze renders ⲉⲡⲃⲓ ⲉⲡⲁⲩⲗⲓⲥ, HABITATIO, COMMORATIO: the Coptic Lexicon of Peyron renders it, VILLA, HABITACULUM, HABITATIO: the Coptic Lexicon of Tattam renders it, ⲉⲡⲁⲩⲗⲓⲥ, HABITACULUM, SEPTUM, CAULA, VILLA, DOMICILIUM, and derives it from a root signifying TRANQUILLITY.

VER. 19.—Whenever God by inspiration calls any individual "*my servant,*" that person is a child of God either by profession of saving faith, or in the eternal purposes of Jehovah. See Note on i. 8. Whenever in the Book of Job any one is called a servant of man, he is so designated in contradistinction from a slave. Slavery was unknown in the days of Job, at least in his vicinity, and as far as mention occurs in this Poem. The world was not then cursed with men-stealers and slave-traders. And if the age of Job was coetaneous and cotemporary with that of Peleg, the world was not then divided, or only recently divided, among the descendants of Noah, and hence slavery could scarcely have then existed. When Noah predicted the future slavery of the descendants of Ham or Canaan, he employs the superlative phrase, "A SERVANT OF SERVANTS shall he be unto his brethren." Even this phrase would go far to prove, that in this Poem a SERVANT is identical with a LABOURER or HIRELING, and does not signify a SLAVE. England and America have righteously abolished slavery and the slave-trade. Their influence with the nations foreshadows the early and entire extinction of African slavery. Now the destinies of the descendants of Shem, Ham, and Japhet, predicted by Noah, extend nearly, if not quite, to the Second Advent. Hence the cessation of the curse, that the descendants of Ham shall be slaves to the descendants of Shem and Japhet, seems another sign of the times, that the Second Advent of Christ in power and great glory is near, even at the doors—"Be ye also ready, for in such an hour as ye think not, the Son of Man cometh."

FIRST SPEECH OF ELIPHAZ THE TEMANITE.

CHAPTERS IV. AND V.

Eliphaz reproves Job for irreligion, laying down the erroneous axiom, that the righteous are UNIVERSALLY *exempt from the judgments judicially inflicted in time upon the wicked.*
The Divine vision communicated to Eliphaz.
God's judicially inflicted judgments upon the persons and the offspring of those who fear and love Him not.
Eliphaz erroneously maintains that temporal prosperity, family mercies, and a blessed longevity are ALWAYS *consequent on God's fatherly corrections, sanctified to His children.*

1 Then responded Eliphaz the Temanite, and said:

2 If argument with thee be assayed, wilt thou be grieved?
   Yet who can refrain from speaking?

3 Behold, thou hast admonished many,
   And the feeble hands thou hast strengthened.

4 Thy words have upheld the stumbling,
   And the trembling knees thou hast sustained.

5 But now it is come upon thee, and thou faintest,
   It smiteth thee, and thou art confounded.

6 Is thy reverence then nothing? thy hope?
   Thy confidence? and the integrity of thy ways?

7 Call to mind, I pray thee, who hath perished, being innocent.
   Or where have the righteous been cut off?

8 According to what I have seen, the ploughers of iniquity
   And the sowers of wickedness reap the same.

9 By the blast of God they perish,
   And by the breath of His nostrils they are consumed.

10 The roaring of the lion, and the yell of the black-maned lion,
    And the teeth of the young lions are dissipated.

11 The strong lion perisheth for lack of prey,
    And the whelps of the lioness are scattered abroad.

12 Now an oracle was secretly imparted to me,
   And mine ear caught a whisper of it,
13 In thoughts perturbed from visions of the night,
   When deep sleep falleth upon men.
14 Palpitation came upon me, and terrors,
   And caused my bones exceedingly to tremble.
15 And a spirit glided before my face,
   The hair of my flesh bristled.
16 It stood still, but I could not discern the form thereof,
   The spectre was stationary before mine eyes,
   And I heard a voice (saying):
17 " Can a mortal be justified before God?
   Can man be pure before his Creator?
18 Behold, He confideth not in His ministers,
   Yea, upon His angels He visits defection;
19 How much more upon inhabiters of houses of clay,
   Whose foundation is in the dust,
   Who are crushed before the moth-worm?
20 They are cut down from morning till evening,
   Utterly they perish, no man regarding it.
21 Doth not their pre-eminence pass away with them?
   They die, verily a nothing in wisdom."

CHAPTER V.

1 Proclaim loudly, I beseech thee, that it is the punishment of thy sin.
  To which indeed of the Holy Ones canst thou appeal?
2 For wrath killeth the fool,
  And indignation slayeth the simple one.
3 I have myself seen the fool take root,
  And instantly I denounced his habitation.
4 Far off are his children from safety,
  And they are crushed at the gate, and no protector.

5 Whose harvest the wild starveling devoureth,
   Even from out of thorns doth he seize it,
   And the wild robber swoopeth up their subsistence.

6 For not from the dust springeth affliction,
   Nor from the ground sprouteth trouble.

7 Behold ! man is born unto trouble,
   As sparks from glowing embers upward wing their flight.

8 Indeed I myself would seek unto God,
   And unto God I would commit my cause.

9 Who doeth things great and unsearchable,
   Things marvellous, surpassing number.

10 Who giveth rain on the face of the earth,
   And sendeth water upon the surface of the pastures.

11 To raise on high the humble,
   And that the mournful may be exalted to safety.

12 Frustrating the devices of the crafty,
   So that their hands cannot perform their enterprise.

13 Entangling the wise in their own craftiness,
   So that the counsel of the perverse is carried headlong.

14 They encounter darkness in the daytime,
   And grope in the noonday as in the night.

15 So he saveth the desolate from their mouth,
   And the helpless from the power of the violent.

16 So there is hope for the destitute,
   And iniquity stoppeth her mouth.

17 Behold ! happy is the man whom God correcteth,
   Therefore despise not thou the chastening of the Almighty.

18 For He bruiseth, and bindeth up,
   He woundeth, and His hands make whole.

19 In six troubles He will deliver thee,
   Yea, in seven evil shall not afflict thee.

20 In famine He shall redeem thee from death,
And in war from the power of the sword.

21 From the scourge of the tongue thou shalt be hid,
And shalt not be afraid of devastation when it cometh.

22 At devastation and famine thou shalt laugh,
And shalt not dread the wild beasts of the earth.

23 Lo! with the stones of the plain shall be thy covenant,
Yea, the wild beasts of the field shall be at peace with thee.

24 So shalt thou prove that thy tabernacle is peace,
And shalt order thine household, and not miscarry.

25 Thou shalt see that thy seed is multitudinous,
And thine offspring as the grass of the earth.

26 In ripe old age shalt thou come to the grave,
As the oblation of a shock of corn in its season.

27 Lo! this we have searched out, so it is.
Hear thou it, and be thou assured of it for thyself.

CHAP. IV. VER. 7. *Call to mind, I pray thee, who hath perished, being innocent.*—It is difficult, if not impossible, to account satisfactorily for Eliphaz's preterition of the murder of Abel by his brother Cain. The Creation and Fall were known to Job and his friend; hence they must also have known of the first death resulting from the fall. This was a more premeditated murder than the Authorized Version in Genesis represents. The Samaritan Pentateuch, the LXX., the Targums of Jerusalem, and Jonathan, Philo, Clemens Romanus, all read: "And Cain said unto Abel his brother, LET US GO INTO THE FIELD, and it came to pass when they were in the field that Cain rose up against his brother, and slew him."—*Genesis* iv. 8. Did Eliphaz pass over this fratricidal murder in the heat of argument, and from over-anxiety to confute Job? Let the error of Eliphaz be a warning to us never, under any circumstances, to misrepresent truth either by unjustifiable additions, perversions, or omissions. Bishop Sanderson has well remarked: "We may not lie for the glory of God."

VER. 12-17.—Before a written revelation was vouchsafed to man, it pleased God frequently to make known His Divine will by dreams and visions of the night. After the word written had been graciously communicated, though only in part, Divine visions and dreams were comparatively infrequent. But spectral visions and admonitory dreams will again be multiplied before the Second Advent as signs and evidences to God's children of the near approach of the glorious Epiphany of Jehovah-Jesus. Joel has thus predicted: "Your sons and your daughters shall prophesy, your old men shall dream dreams, your young men shall see visions" (ii. 28). Joel was the prophet and the mouthpiece of God. And what Joel has foretold, God, in fulfilment of His everlasting covenant in all things ordered and sure, will fulfil in His own time, and according to His infinite wisdom. As Divine visions were communicated to Abraham, Daniel, Peter, Paul, and Cornelius, and admonitory dreams to Abimelech, Jacob, Laban, Joseph, Pharaoh, Pharaoh's Chief-Butler and Baker, Solomon, Nebuchadnezzar, and Daniel, so an oracular vision was vouchsafed to Eliphaz to humble his soul in the dust, and to teach him, that before the omniscient heart-searching Creator, and in His sight, no man living can be justified.

VER. 21. *Pre-eminence.*—Man's pre-eminence is that dominion over the world which God granted to Adam and Eve in paradise. "And God said, Let us make man in our image, after our likeness; and let them have dominion over the fish of the sea, and over the fowl of the air, and over the cattle, and over all the earth, and over every creeping thing that creepeth upon the earth. So God created man in His own image, in the image of God created He him; male and female created He them. And God blessed them, and said unto them: Be fruitful and multiply, and replenish the earth, and subdue it: and have dominion over the fish of the sea, and over the fowl of the air, and over every living thing that moveth upon the earth" (*Genesis* i. 26-28). This dominion God renewed to Noah and his descendants: "And the fear of you, and the dread of you, shall be upon every beast of the earth, and upon every fowl of the air, upon all that moveth upon the earth, and upon all the fishes of the sea; into your hand are they delivered" (*Genesis* ix. 2). This dominion and pre-eminence over the earth and animal creation is only co-existent with human life. "When man dieth, he shall carry nothing away; his glory shall not descend after him. He shall go to the generation of his fathers; they shall never see light. Man being in honour abideth not; he is like the beasts that perish" (*Psalm* xlix. 17, 19, 20). This dominion is an earnest and prelude of millennial pre-eminence, which the risen glorified saints shall exercise, when they shall be made kings and priests ON THE EARTH (*Revelation* xx. 6), and shall take the kingdom and possess the kingdom for ever. "Thou madest him to have dominion over the works of Thy hands; Thou hast put all things under his feet: all sheep and oxen, yea, and the beasts of the field, the fowl of the air, and the fish of the sea, and whatsoever passeth through the paths of the seas" (*Psalm* viii. 6-8).

CHAP. V. VER. 1. *The Holy Ones*.—"Jehovah, being three Persons, each equally holy, great, uncreate, unbegotten, co-eternal."—*Bates' Hebrew Lexicon*. "HOLY in the singular number is often applied to Jehovah, and denotes His being entirely separated from all evil and defilement.—See Lev. xi. 44, 45; xix. 2. Compare Isa. vi. 3. So in the plural number it is joined with the Hebrew plural for God (Joshua xxiv. 19). Compare Daniel iv. 5, 6, 15 (or 8, 9, 18), and thus the plural noun by itself signifies THE HOLY ONES, *i.e.*, THE HOLY PERSONS OF THE TRINITY, Proverbs ix. 10, where observe, that, according to the usual style of Hebrew poetry, THE HOLY ONES in the latter hemistich corresponds to JEHOVAH in the former."—(*Parkhurst's Hebrew Lexicon*. The meaning of this first verse is: Confess boldly and openly that thy sufferings are the merited punishment of thy sin, for to which of the three Persons of the eternal Trinity canst thou appeal in vindication of thy innocence, seeing that Jehovah hath afflicted thee, and that this thine affliction is the proof and result of His cognisance of thy sin?

REPLY OF JOB TO THE FIRST SPEECH OF ELIPHAZ.

CHAPTERS VI. AND VII.

The severity of Job's sufferings causeth him to wish for death, assured, as he was, that death would be productive to him of consolation and joy.

Job bemoans the absence of all commiseration, and denounces the hollowness of the reproofs of his friend.

Job recapitulates his heavy affliction, on account of which he preferred death to life. He confesseth to God his sinfulness, and entreats pardon from his heavenly Father in anticipation of death, the annihilation of his body in the grave, and its reanimation on the morning of the resurrection—the first resurrection—the resurrection to millennial glory.

1 Then responded Job, and said:

2 O that my grief were thoroughly weighed,
And my calamity simultaneously placed in the balances!

3 For now would it be heavier than the sand of the sea,
Therefore my words have been inconsiderate.

4 Behold, the arrows of the Almighty are within me,
   The poison whereof drinketh up my spirit;
   The terrors of God set themselves in array against me.

5 Doth the wild ass bray over tender herbage?
   Or loweth the ox over his fodder?

6 Can that which is insipid be eaten without salt?
   Is there flavour in the froth of camel's milk?

7 My soul hath loathed to taste them,
   They are to me as polluted food.

8 O that my request might be fulfilled,
   And that God would grant my earnest desire!

9 Yea, that it would please God to destroy me!
   That He would redouble His hand, and cut me off!

10 Then at length I should have consolation,
    Then should I exult for joy. Let Him not spare me;
    Truly I have not rejected the words of the Holy One!

11 What is my strength, that I should have hope?
    And what is my end, that I should prolong my life?

12 Is my strength the strength of stones?
    Is my flesh brass?

13 Is it not, that there is no help for me in myself,
    And that duration of life is expelled far from me?

14 To the afflicted pity should be showed from his friend,
    Although he have forsaken the fear of the Almighty.

15 My brethren have dealt deceitfully as a wady,
    Like wady-streams they have passed away.

16 They flow turbid by reason of the ice,
    The snow foams above them.

17 What time they wax warm they evaporate,
    When it is hot, they are dried up out of their place.

18 The courses of their current are devious,
    They go to nothing, and are lost.

19 The caravans of Tema looked out wistfully,
   The companies of Sheba earnestly expected them.

20 They were confounded, because they had been confident;
   They proceeded hitherto, and were covered with confusion.

21 Behold, now ye are a nothing,
   Ye see my downcasting, and are afraid.

22 Is it that I have said : " Come give me ?"
   Or " Present unto me of your wealth ?"

23 Or " Rescue me out of the hand of an enemy ?"
   Or " Redeem me from the hand of the violent ?"

24 Instruct me, and I will keep silence,
   Yea, cause me to understand wherein I have erred.

25 How forcible are right arguments !
   But how doth the reproof from you reprove ?

26 Do ye indeed devise words to reprove ?
   Even (to reprove) the empty speeches of one in despair ?

27 Yea, ye vent your anger upon the destitute,
   And dig (a pitfall) for your friend.

28 But now, be ye willing, turn ye towards me,
   And before your faces (it shall be seen) that I lie not.

29 Turn again, I beseech you, let there be no offence,
   Yea, turn again, here is my justification.

30 Is there unrighteousness in my tongue ?
   Cannot my taste discern perverse things ?

CHAPTER VII.

1 Is there not to man an appointed warfare upon earth ?
  And are not his days as the days of an hireling ?

2 Like a servant he panteth for the night shade,
  And like an hireling he longeth for his wages.

3 So am I made to possess months of misery,
  And wearisome nights are appointed to me.

4 If I lie down, then I exclaim :
"When shall I arise, and the eventide be gone ?"
And I am full of tossings unto day-dawn.

5 My flesh is clothed with worms and adhesions of dust,
My skin is rigid, and become loathsome.

6 Swifter than a weaver's shuttle are my days,
And they are ended from rupture of the thread.

7 Remember that my life is a puff of wind,
Never again shall my eye see good.

8 The eye of him that hath seen me shall see me no more ;
Thine eyes are upon me, and I am not.

9 The cloud is dissolved, and vanisheth away,
So he that descendeth to Sheol shall never ascend.

10 No more shall he return to his house,
And his dwelling-place shall know him no more.

11 Yea, verily I myself will not refrain my mouth,
I will speak in the anguish of my spirit,
In the bitterness of my soul I will complain (saying) :

12 "Am I a sea or a sea monster,
That thou shouldest appoint a keeper over me ?"

13 When I say, "My bed shall comfort me,
My couch shall alleviate my complaint,"

14 Then dost Thou scare me with dreams,
And terrify me with visions.

15 So that my soul coveteth suffocation,
Death in preference to my skeleton-life.

16 I waste away, I would not live always ;
Cease Thou from me, for my days are a vapour.

17 What is man, that Thou shouldest magnify him ?
And that Thou shouldest set Thine heart upon him ?

18 And that Thou shouldest visit him morning after morning,
And prove him moment after moment ?

19 Why then wilt Thou not turn away Thine eyes from me?
Why wilt Thou not leave me alone, till I can swallow my spittle?

20 I have sinned, What shall I do unto Thee, O Thou supervisor of men?
Why hast Thou set me up as a target before Thee,
So that I am become a burden to myself?

21 And why dost Thou not take away my transgression?
And why dost Thou not cause my sin to pass away?

For soon shall I lie down in the dust,
And in the morning Thou shalt seek me, but I shall be no more.

CHAP. VI. VER. 6. *Camel's milk.*—Michaelis strongly advocates CAMEL'S MILK as the proper rendering of the Hebrew noun, which occurs in no other passage of the Old Testament Scriptures. He affirms that CAMEL'S MILK, when first drawn, has much froth, which subsides only after some hours; and that the Arabs, accustomed to milk camels, deduce many proverbs from the frothiness of the milk, comparing anger, ostentation, vanity, and whatever is superficial and not solid, with this insipid and innutritious froth. See Michaelis Sup. ad Lex. Heb., pp. 779 and 780. Castell declares that the corresponding Arabic term in two formations signifies A FAT CAMEL. Kitto testifies to the general use of CAMEL'S MILK. "CAMEL'S MILK at present is much used by the Arabs. It is the milk for drink, that of the goats and sheep being generally made into butter. Even the young horse-colts, after being weaned, are fed exclusively on camel's milk for a considerable time, and in some tribes the adult horses partake of it largely. Flour made into a paste, with *sour* camel's milk, is a standing dish among the Bedouins. Rice or flour boiled with sweet camel's milk is another."—*History of Palestine,* ii. 390.

VER. 12. *Brass.*—" It has been usual in all ages to mix up copper with other metals, for greater convenience in working, and for superior qualities which it thus acquires. One of these mixed metals connected with copper is bronze, and this was extensively employed in ancient times, and it may strictly be the metal intended in many parts of Scripture. It is ascertained that the Egyptians, at an early period, were well acquainted with working in bronze, and it is most likely that what are called brazen vessels in the Books of Moses were really of bronze;—this rather than simple copper, because bronze is less liable to tarnish, and takes on a finer polish; and rather bronze than brass, because zinc, which forms a component element in brass, does not, as far as yet discovered, appear to have been known to the ancients."—*Fairbairn's Imperial Dictionary.* "The skill of the Egyptians in compounding metals is abundantly proved by the vases, mirrors, arms, and implements of bronze discovered at Thebes, and other parts of Egypt; and the numerous methods they adopted for varying the composition of bronze by a judicious admixture of alloys, are shown in the many qualities of the metal. They had even the secret of giving to bronze or brass blades a certain degree of elasticity, as may be seen in the dagger of the Berlin Museum, already noticed, which probably depended on the mode of hammering the metal, and the just proportions of peculiar alloys. Another remarkable feature in their bronze is the resistance it offers to the effect of the atmosphere, some continuing sweet and bright though buried for ages, and since exposed to the damp of European climates, and some presenting the appearance of previous oxidation purposely induced."—*Wilkinson's Ancient Egyptians.* " Brass is used sometimes as the symbol of incorrigible pride and wanton immorality, and sometimes as an emblem of durability and strength."—*Eadie.*

VER. 14.—Commiseration of the fallen, more especially when sin has been visited by retributive justice, is in this verse earnestly and righteously enjoined by Job; yet how generally neglected by God's children is this commanded duty! How reluctant are we to ask our own hearts, "What hath made us to differ?" How many opportunities of intercessory prayer, sympathetic admonition, mild reproof, have passed by unheeded and disregarded! Who, taking a retrospect of his past life, will not have cause to mourn over his defects of duty to God and man in this respect! How often have caustic censures pre-occupied our hearts, and expelled therefrom sympathy, commiseration, and intercession! An old writer well remarked, "If sorrow can enter heaven, it will be because we have done so little for Christ on earth."

CHAP. VII. VERS. 9, 10.—These verses indisputably prove, that the dead return not to this earth, nor ever manifest themselves to the living. No intercommunication exists between disembodied spirits and the living yet in a state of probation on earth. The Church militant and the Church triumphant are sundered by an impassable gulph, and will never be reunited till after the first resurrection, and the establishment of Christ's millennial kingdom upon earth. We are living under an inspired revelation of God's will never vouchsafed to Job. We are privileged with the meridian blaze of gospel light, which Job only contemplated through the distant vista of futurity. We are living in the days of the Son of Man, which Job desired to see, but saw not. Yet notwithstanding all the light, knowledge, and privileges possessed by this generation, the sins of spiritualism, table-turning, and supposititious intercommunication with departed spirits, unknown and unpractised in the days of Job, now abound, are vindicated, and gloried in. Job and his patriarchal contemporaries were not guilty of these abominations. Intercommunication with the dead, in all its forms, phases, and pretences, in England, America, and New Zealand, is DIABOLISM.

VER. 15. *Coveteth suffocation.*—Bridel states "LA DIFFICULTÉ D'AVALER," to be one of the painful symptoms of the elephantiasis. So that when Job coveted suffocation, he coveted death in that form, and from that cause, generally, and perhaps most generally, resulting from the elephantiasis. (See Note on the Elephantiasis on ii. 7.)

VER. 21. *In the morning.*—That is, in the commencement of Christ's millennial kingdom upon earth, when will be the first resurrection, the glorious resurrection of all departed saints, and the glorious change of all saints who shall then be living on the earth. The first resurrection, the resurrection to glory, will take place at the beginning or morning of the great Day of God Almighty. The second resurrection, the resurrection of the lost, will take place at the termination of Christ's millennial kingdom and glory. The language of Job asserts his assurance, that he should participate in the bliss and glories of the first resurrection—(see the Author's translation of Psalm xlix. 14 in his *Psalterium Messianicum Davidis Regis et Prophetæ*),—although his body should have returned to its original dust.

"Thy dead shall live again;
The dead of my people shall arise,
Awake and sing, ye that dwell in the dust!
For Thy dew is as the dew upon herbs,
And the earth shall cast forth her dead."—*Isaiah* xxvi. 19, *by Barnes.*

FIRST SPEECH OF BILDAD THE SHUHITE.

CHAPTER VIII.

Bildad asserts:
That afflictions are God's judgments upon the ungodly;
That the children of Job by evil deeds deserved their premature death;
That secular prosperity is the necessary concomitant of true religion.

This fallacious argument Bildad endeavours to substantiate by quotations from ancient patriarchal sayings anterior to the age of Job—proverbial sayings, abstractedly true, but not applicable to the case of Job—proverbial sayings current in the East far more than 4000 years ago, conserved and transmitted to us in this the most ancient book extant in the world, the first written revelation God ever vouchsafed to the children of men.

1 Then responded Bildad the Shuhite, and said:

2 How long wilt thou affirm these things?
And the words of thy mouth be a tempestuous wind?

3 Will God pervert judgment?
　Or will the Almighty pervert justice?

4 Though thy children have sinned against Him,
　And He hath cast them away on account of their trangressions,

5 If thou wouldest seek betimes unto God,
　And make thy supplication unto the Almighty;

6 If thou be pure and upright,
　Surely now He would arise for thee,
　And would make prosperous the habitation of thy righteousness.

7 Although thy beginning be small,
　Yet thy latter end should be greatly exalted.

8 Therefore inquire, I pray thee, of the former generation,
　Yea, apply thyself to the examination of their forefathers:

9 For we are but of yesterday, and know nothing,
　For a shadow are our days upon the earth.

10 Shall they not instruct thee? They speak unto thee,
　And out of their wisdom well forth proverbs.

11 Can the papyrus shoot majestically without ooze?
　Can the reed-grass grow up to an height without water?

12 Even yet in the midst of its greenness, uncut,
　And before all other herbage, it withereth.

13 Such are the courses of all that forget God,
　So perishes the hope of the profane.

14 Whose reliance shall be cut off,
　And whose confidence shall be the spider's web,

15 Which resteth upon his web, but it shall not stand,
　Which holdeth it fast, but it shall not abide.

16 He is verdant before the sun riseth,
　And his branches shoot over his garden.

17 Among a stone-heap shall his roots be intertwined,
   At a bed of stones shall they be seen.

18 Its native soil absorbs it from its place,
   And shall renounce it (saying): "I have never seen thee!"

19 Lo! such is the joy of his course!
   And others sprout forth from his dust.

20 Lo! God will not cast away the sincere,
   Neither will He strengthen the hand of evil-doers.

21 Even yet may He fill thy mouth with laughter,
   And thy lips with exultation.

22 They that hate thee shall be clothed with shame,
   And the tent of the reprobates shall be no more.

CHAP. VIII. VERS. 11. *Papyrus.*—"This plant is without doubt the celebrated papyrus of Egypt, the first material used in the manufacture of paper, which thence derives its name—the *Cyperus Papyrus* of botanists belonging to the Sedge family. It formerly abounded in the Nile, flourishing in the mire, in which Job describes it, and is represented by ancient writers as forming a complete forest on its banks. Now it is wholly extinct in Egypt, and is no longer found in Africa, excepting in marshes of the White Nile in Nubia, 7° north latitude. But while extirpated there, it still lingers in two spots in Palestine, the only places in Asia where it occurs. It grows very luxuriantly in a swamp at the north end of the Plain of Gennesaret, close to the fountain of Ain-et-Tin, and it covers many acres in the inaccessible marshes of the Huleh, the ancient Merom, and is known to the Arabs by its old name 'Babeer,' of which papyrus is simply the Latinized form. It is a beautiful and graceful plant, and flourishes in stagnant swamps, or in deep soft mud. Its renown arises from its having supplied the earliest known paper."—*Tristram's Natural History of the Bible,* pp. 433, 435.

"The papyrus extends right across from the west to the east end of the Huleh. A false step off its roots will take the intruder over head in suffocating peat mud. We spent a long time in attempting to effect an entrance, and at last gave it up, satisfied that the marsh birds were not to be had. In fact the whole is simply a floating bog of several miles square—a very thin crust of vegetation over an unknown depth of water, and if the weight of the explorer breaks through this, suffocation is imminent. Some of the Arabs, who were tilling the plain for cotton, assured us, that even a wild boar never got through it. We shot two bitterns, but, in endeavouring to retrieve them, I slipped from the root on which I was standing, and was drawn down in a moment, only saving myself from drowning by my gun, which had providentially caught across a papyrus stem."—*The Land of Israel, by Tristram,* p. 587.

VER. 11. *Reed-grass.*—"From the passage in Job, where the bulrush is named with the papyrus, there can be little doubt but some specific plant is intended, and from Genesis xli. 2 and 18, it must have been one eaten by the cattle. The word is Egyptian, and not Hebrew. The *Cyperus esculentus,* or edible rush, and the *Butomus umbellatus,* the beautiful Flowering Rush, would either meet the requirements of the sacred text."—*Tristram's Natural History of the Bible.* p. 435.

Peyron in his Lexicon of the Coptic language affirms, that ACHU, the name by which Job designates the REED GRASS, is a generic term, and signifies all the green herbage of every description growing in marshes: "Ægyptiis, hoc nomine linguâ eorum omne quod in palude virens nascitur, appellatur."

REPLY OF JOB TO THE FIRST SPEECH OF BILDAD.

CHAPTERS IX. AND X.

Job asserts the sovereignty of God in the administration of the universe and of human affairs, and acknowledges Jehovah's mysterious permission of Satan, the God of this world, and Prince of the power of the air. Job admits his own innate sinfulness and defective obedience, and prays for dismissal from life and liberation from present evils.

1 Then responded Job, and said :
2 Of a truth I know that it is so :
   But how can mortal man be justified before God ?
3 If He vouchsafe to enter into litigation with him,
   He cannot answer Him one charge of a thousand.
4 Wise in understanding and strong in power,
   Who hath hardened himself against Him, and prospered ?
5 Who removeth mountains, and men are not conscious
   Who in His anger hath overturned them :
6 Who causeth the vibration of the earth out of its place,
   So that the columns thereof recoil :
7 Who commandeth the sun, and it riseth not,
   And setteth His seal upon the stars :
8 Who alone stretcheth out the heavens,
   And walketh upon the depths of the sea :
9 Who created Ash (the polar star), Cesil (the brumal constellation),
   Cimah (the vernal constellation), and the unseen southern heavens.
10 He doeth great things surpassing research,
   Yea, wonders surpassing description.
11 Lo ! He passeth over me, and I see Him not,
   And He glideth by, and I perceive Him not.
12 Lo ! He taketh away, and who can make Him restore ?
   Who can say to Him, " What doest Thou ? "

13 God will not turn away His anger;
   Beneath Him are prostrate the supports of pride.
14 How much less can I argue with Him,
   (And) arrange my pleadings against Him?
15 With whom, though I were innocent, I would not argue,
   I would make supplication to my judge.
16 Should I call, and He should respond to me,
   I could not believe that He had hearkened to my voice.
17 He who is overwhelming me with a tempest,
   And is multiplying my wounds without cause.
18 He suffereth me not to refresh my spirit,
   But surfeiteth me with bitter things.
19 If I appeal to MIGHT, lo! how powerful is He?
   And if to JUDGMENT, who would become a witness for me?
20 Should I justify myself, my own mouth would condemn me;
   (If I say,) I am sincere, it would even prove me perverse.
21 I know not perfection:
   (If I did,) I myself should disown my own being.
22 Nevertheless this one truth I affirm,
   He destroyeth both the sincere and the wicked.
23 If He suddenly slay the oppressor,
   He derideth the trials of the innocent.
24 The earth is given over to the hand of the wicked one,
   Who hoodwinketh the faces of its judges.
   If this be not so, where, who is HE?
25 Lo! swifter than a courier are my days,
   They flee away, they witness no good.
26 They pass onward like reed-skiffs,
   Like the eagle pouncing on his prey.
27 If I should say, I will forget all my cares,
   I will change my countenance, and will take consolation to myself,
28 Then I shudder at all my griefs.

I know thou wilt not hold me innocent,
29 I am denounced guilty, why labour I thus in vain?

30 Should I wash myself in snow-waters,
And cleanse my hands with alkali,

31 Still Thou wilt plunge me into the mire,
So that my own clothes would make me to be abhorred.

32 For He is not a man as I am, that I should contend with Him,
And that we should come together into judgment.

33 There is no umpire between us,
Who might lay his hand upon both.

34 Let Him remove from me His rod,
And let not His terror affright me.

35 I would speak and not be afraid of Him,
But not thus can I in my present state.

CHAPTER X.

1 I myself am weary of my life,
I will let loose from myself my complainings,
In the bitterness of my soul I will speak.

2 I will say unto God, Pronounce me not guilty,
Make me to know wherefore Thou contendest with me.

3 Is it befitting Thee that Thou shouldest oppress,
That Thou shouldest despise the work of Thy hands,
And shine upon the counsel of the wicked?

4 Hast Thou eyes of flesh?
Or seest Thou as man seeth?

5 Are Thy days as the days of a mortal?
Are Thy years as the days of man?

6 That Thou searchest after mine iniquity,
And makest inquisition for my sin.

7 With Thy knowledge that I am not a reprobate,
And that none can deliver out of Thine hand.

8 Thine hands have formed me,
   And made me compact in every part,
   And wilt thou utterly destroy me?

9 Remember, I beseech Thee, that as clay Thou hast moulded me,
   And wilt return me again to dust.

10 Hast Thou poured me out like milk?
   And as cheese concreted me together?

11 With skin and flesh Thou hast clothed me,
   And with bones and sinews Thou hast compacted me.

12 Life and favour Thou hast granted me,
   And Thy presiding care hath preserved my spirit.

13 And these things Thou hast hid in Thy heart,
   I know that this was Thy purpose.

14 If I sin, Thou markest me,
   And from mine iniquity Thou wilt not absolve me.

15 If I be a reprobate, woe unto me,
   And if I be righteous, I cannot lift up my head,

   Filled with ignominy, and saturated with my humiliation,
16 Which increaseth upon me.

   As a black-maned lion Thou huntest me,
   And again magnifiest Thyself against me.

17 Thou renewest Thy demonstrations against me,
   And increasest Thine indignation upon me:
   Successive assaults and war are present with me.

18 Wherefore then didst Thou bring me forth from the womb?
   I might have expired, and no eye have seen me.

19 I might have been as though I had never existed,
   I might have been borne from the womb to the grave.

20 Will my few days never pass away?
   Let Him withdraw from me that I may have some consolation
21 Before I shall go whence I shall not return,

To the land of darkness and death-shade,
22 To the land of dissolution, as to utter extinction.

To death-shade where are no rays of light,
And whose shining is as utter extinction.

CHAP. IX. VER. 6. *Columns.*—The Hebrew word rendered PILLARS in our Authorized Version, and COLUMNS by me, is the same term whereby inspiration designates THE PILLAR OF FIRE AND PILLAR OF CLOUD, which conducted the children of Israel out of Egypt, and for forty years regulated all their marches and encampments, sheltering them from the heat of the sun by day, and protecting them from assaults of men or beasts by night, whilst traversing the deserts of Arabia. In that pillar of fire and cloud Christ, the uncreated Angel of the everlasting covenant, was present as He was in the bush of the wilderness, which burned with fire and was not consumed. That presence of Christ with the natural Israel is an emblem and guarantee of His covenanted presence with the spiritual Israel in all their conflicts with the powers of darkness. " Lo, I am with you always, even to the end of the world." The COLUMNS of this verse signify the aërial clouds and effluxes, which cause, or regulate, or accompany the rotation of this globe on its axis, and in its orbit round the sun. This verse seems to refer to some change in the position of this globe, and of its circumambient atmosphere at the era of the Noachian deluge.

VER. 9. *Ash, Cesil, and Cimah.*—Our Authorized Version, following the LXX., renders these words Arcturus, Orion, and Pleiades. To this rendering it may be objected—1*st*, That ancient as the LXX. Version is, it was made not less than 1700 years after this poem was written. Whence did the LXX. translators derive this knowledge? By what channel of tradition was it handed down to them? What means of discovery did they possess which we possess not? 2*d*, The LXX. is self-contradictory, and hence is not implicitly to be relied on.

The LXX. render Ash, Pleiades, ⎫　　⎧ Hesperus, ⎫
　　　　　　　　Cesil, Hesperus, ⎬ ix. 9, ⎨ Orion, ⎬ xxxviii. 32.
　　　　　　　　Cimah, Arcturus, ⎭　　⎩ Pleiades, ⎭

3*d*, This rendering implies, contrary to all probability, that the Signs of the Zodiac and the different constellations were designated above 4000 years ago by the same names they now bear. 4*th*, Were this implication well founded, the Arabic lexicons would give to Ash, Cesil, and Cimah the same significations which the LXX. attribute to them. This is not the fact. Parkhurst, on the contrary, renders Ash, THE BLIGHT; Cesil, THE COLD; and Cimah, GENIAL WARMTH. The version of Parkhurst approximates to the truth, but is scarcely appropriate to the context of these two passages, both of which refer to the sidereal heavens. I have, therefore, substantially followed in both passages the version of Schultens, the most accurate and successful interpreter of this most ancient poem, and consider ASH to designate the Polar Star, which makes its diurnal circuit round the Pole every twenty-four hours; CESIL, to designate the brumal or winter constellation; and CIMAH, the vernal or summer constellation. See, in the Critical Appendix, Schultens's version of these two passages, and the significations in Arabic of ASH, CESIL, and CIMAH, also the observation of the learned Michaelis, who calls the Polar Star MATER STELLARUM, and affirms that it is visible during the whole night and the whole year in Syria, Palestine, Arabia, and Egypt. Schultens considers ASH etymologically to signify, in Arabic, the circum-rotation of the Polar Star; and Dick says: " The Polar Star is somewhat more than a degree and a half from the polar point, and revolves around that point in a small circle every twenty-four hours."—*Celestial Scenery*, p. 26.

VER. 24. *The earth is given over to the hand of the Wicked One.*—This affirmation of Job, resulting from his own painful experience of the buffetings of Satan, seems uttered by him under the afflatus of Divine inspiration. It is fully substantiated by the inspired declarations, that Satan is the God and Prince of this world, working in the children of disobedience (2 *Corinthians* iv. 4; *John* xii. 31, xiv. 30, xvi. 11; *Ephesians* vi. 12); that he is the Prince of the power of the air (*Ephesians* ii. 2). And more especially is Satan's usurped dominion of the world demonstrated by his showing to the Son of Man all the kingdoms of the world, and the glory of them, and by his saying: " All this power will I give Thee, and the glory of them, for that is delivered unto me, and to whomsoever I give it" (*Matthew* iv. 1-11; *Luke* iv. 1-13). Satan was indeed a liar and a murderer from the beginning. He told unto Eve the first lie: " Ye shall not surely die" (*Genesis* iii. 4), and he is the father of lies. But before whom did the fallen spirit claim the autocracy of the world by the mysterious permission of

God? He claimed it in the presence of the omniscient, prescient Messiah, who knoweth the end from the beginning, even in the presence of Jehovah-Jesus, perfect God as well as perfect man. Hence we infer that Satan, who by mysterious permission tempted Job, despoiled him of his property and children, and afflicted him with the burning ulceration of the loathsome elephantiasis, exercises mysteriously permitted autocracy over the four world-wide dynasties foreshown to Nebuchadnezzar and Daniel in dreams and visions of the night, and vividly depicted by the prophet in two similitudes, during their predicted duration of 2520 years from the birth of Nebuchadnezzar till the consummation of the times of the Gentiles. The present manifest increase of Satanic influence over the hearts of the unregenerate seems one sign of our approximation to that final earthquake and that final crash of nations, which will immediately precede and usher in the glorious Epiphany of Jehovah-Jesus. Satan is now unwontedly active, because his time is short.

CHAP. X. VER. 10.—" Mine embryo substance Thou like milk didst pour,
And then condense it to the shape it bore."—*Stather.*

" From the well-tempered or mingled MILK of the chyle, every individual atom of every individual organ in the human frame, the most compact and consolidated, as well as the soft and pliable, is perpetually supplied and renewed, through the medium of a set of LACTEALS or MILK-VESSELS, as they are usually called in anatomy, from the nature of this common chyle or milk which they circulate. It circulates through the system, and either continues fluid as milk in its simple state, or is rendered solid, as milk in its caseous or cheese state, according to the nature of the organ which it supplies with its vital current."—*John Mason Good, M.D.*

FIRST SPEECH OF ZOPHAR THE NAAMATHITE.

CHAPTER XI.

Zophar condemns the arguments of Job, charges him with sin, and affirms that his present suffering was God's judicial infliction for his past iniquities. He exhorteth to reformation, and amendment, and repentance, that his sins might be blotted out.

1 Then responded Zophar the Naamathite, and said :

2 Shall a multitude of words not be answered ?
   Or shall a man of much talk be (thereby) justified ?

3 Shall thy self-sufficiency make men to be silent ?
   Or shalt thou mock, and no one put thee to shame ?

4 Yea, thou hast said : " My doctrine is pure
   And I am clean in Thine eyes."

5 But, O that God would speak,
   And open His lips against thee !

6 And that He would reveal to thee the deep mysteries of wisdom,
   That they are the counterparts of sound reason,
   And the knowledge that God hath made thee His debtor because
   of thine iniquity.

7 Canst thou by searching find out God ?
   Canst thou find out the Almighty to perfection ?

8 O the heights of heaven! What canst thou do?
　O the depth below Sheol! What canst thou understand?

9 The measure thereof is longer than the earth,
　And wider than the sea.

10 If he attack, or imprison,
　Or summon to judgment, who then can change Him?

11 Behold, He discerneth men of falsehood,
　And seeth iniquity; and shall He not notice it?

12 Let then the hollow-hearted man become wise,
　And the wild-ass colt be regenerated a man.

13 If thou prepare thine heart,
　And spread out thine hands towards Him,

14 If the iniquity which is in thine hands thou put far away,
　And suffer not wickedness to abide in thy tents.

15 Lo! then shalt thou lift up thy face without spot,
　And firm shalt thou be, and shalt not fear.

16 Then shalt thou forget affliction,
　As waters which have passed away shalt thou remember it.

17 And thy life shall rise brighter than the noon-day,
　Thou shalt shine forth, thou shalt be resplendent as the morning.

18 And thou shalt be confident, for substantial shall be thy hope,
　And though now confounded, yet shalt thou repose in security.

19 Yea, thou shalt lie down, and none shall make thee afraid,
　And many shall make their suit unto thee.

20 But the eyes of the wicked shall waste away,
　And escape shall utterly fail them,
　And their hope shall be an expiring breath.

CHAP. XI. VER. 8. *Sheol.*—SHEOL occurs eight times in the poem of Job, in this verse and in vii. 9, xiv. 13, xvii. 13, 16, xxi. 13, xxiv. 19, xxvi. 6.
　　vii. 9. —The cloud is dissolved, and vanisheth away,
　　　　So he that descendeth to SHEOL shall never ascend.
　　xiv. 13.—O that thou wouldest secrete me in SHEOL!
　　xvii. 13.—Lo! I await SHEOL to be my home,
　　　　I have spread my bed in the darkness.
　　xvii. 16.—To the depths of SHEOL Thou makest them to descend.
　　　　Verily to the dust shall all descend together.

xxi. 13.—In prosperity they spend their days,
  And in a moment are brought down to SHEOL.
xxiv. 19.—Drought and heat consume the snow-waters,
  So does SHEOL those who have sinned.
xxvi. 6.—SHEOL is naked before Him,
  And Perdition hath no covering.

SHEOL signifies the receptacle of departed spirits both saved and lost. This receptacle is beneath the crust of the earth, to which all spirits at death descend. In this receptacle, immediately after death, the souls of the saved repose on Abraham's bosom, and the souls of the lost are in incipient torment. And in this receptacle the souls of believers remain until the first resurrection, when, raised from Sheol, they shall reign with Christ one thousand years on earth, and the souls of unbelievers remain till the one thousand years of Christ's reign on earth shall be completed, and Christ shall judge the quick and dead.

Scott, the author of the Book of Job in English verse, thus summarizes what is written of SHEOL in the Book of Job:—

"First, SHEOL is represented to be a portion of space, vast and deep.

"Secondly, SHEOL is spoken of as the common receptacle of human souls after death.

"Job desired earnestly to be there, the wicked also go down thither.

"Thirdly, this region of disembodied spirits seems to be placed in the bowels of the earth under the great abyss.

"I apprehend that xxvi. 5, 6 not only determines the situation of SHEOL, but also implies that wicked souls are in a state of suffering there, and consequently are separated from the good, whose residence therefore is supposed to be in a different part of this subterraneous region.

"It seems to have been a very ancient opinion among the Hebrews, that the dwelling of unbodied souls is within the earth; for in 1 Samuel xxviii. 13, the witch of Endor says to Saul, I saw the judge (Samuel) ascending OUT OF THE EARTH."

VER. 16.—*As waters which have passed away.*—Arabia has no rivers, and Palestine only the Jordan. Both countries are fertilized by water-courses, of which some few are perennial, but by far the greater part are mere winter-torrents, inundating the valleys in winter, but dry in summer in whole or in part. These winter-torrents are now commonly called wadys. Their number may be estimated by the circumstance, that Tristram, in his *Land of Israel*, enumerates 42; Stanley, in his *Sinai and Palestine*, 48; and Wilson, in his *Lands of the Bible*, 85. In Robinson's *Researches in Palestine*, the word WADY is of constant occurrence. THE WATERS WHICH HAVE PASSED AWAY are the wadys of Arabia and Palestine, which roar tumultuously in the winter, and dash down the ravines, and sweep away every obstruction, but evaporate in the summer, or are absorbed in the sands of the desert. An apt similitude to assure Job that, as the roaring wadys of summer disappear in the winter, so on his contrition his present grief should be made to pass away to be remembered no more for ever.

REPLY OF JOB TO THE FIRST SPEECH OF ZOPHAR.

CHAPTERS XII., XIII., AND XIV.

The affliction of Job contrasted with the prosperity of the wicked.
The sovereignty of God in the administration of the universe.

Job reproveth the partiality of the argumentation of his friends, professeth confidence in God as HIS GOD, *confesseth his sinfulness, and prays for a revelation of his own sins, and of the gracious purpose of God in his affliction.*

The brevity of human life resulting from Adam's transgression. The dead return no more to this earth, and are not conscious of mundane affairs, until the first resurrection of the elect to glory at the Second Advent of Christ.

1 Then responded Job, and said:

2 Doubtless ye are the people,
  And wisdom shall die with you!

3 But I have understanding as well as you,
  I fall nothing short of you,
  And with whom are not such sayings as these?

4 I am one who is a laughing-stock to his neighbour,
  Who calleth upon God, and He answereth him:
  The righteous sincere man is a laughing-stock.

5 He that is ready to slip with his foot
  Is a castaway torch amidst the sunshine of the prosperous.

6 The tents of the spoilers are in tranquillity,
  Yea, they are refuges to them who provoke God,
  Even Him, who hath brought into being all these things.

7 But ask now the beasts, and they shall teach thee,
  And the birds of the air, and they shall tell thee;

8 Or speak to the earth, and it shall teach thee,
  And the fishes of the sea shall declare to thee.

9 Who among all these knoweth not
  That the hand of Jehovah doeth this?

10 In whose hand is the breath of every living creature
   And the spirit of all human flesh.

11 Should not the ear test words,
   As the palate for itself tastes food?

12 Is wisdom with the aged?
   And understanding with length of days?

13 With Him are wisdom and power,
   To Him pertain counsel and understanding.

14 Behold, He demolisheth, and it cannot be rebuilt,
   He shutteth up a man, and none can release him.

15 Behold, He restraineth the waters, and they are dried up.
   And He sendeth them forth, and they desolate the earth.

16 With Him are strength and wisdom,
   The misled and misleader are His.

17 Counsellors He leadeth away captive,
   And judges He infatuates.
18 He subverts the authority of kings,
   And with a servile belt He bindeth their loins.
19 Princes He leadeth away captive,
   And the mighty He prostrates.
20 He taketh away the eloquence of rulers,
   And removeth the discernment of elders.
21 He poureth contempt upon princes,
   And looseneth the girdle of the mighty.
22 He discloseth the recesses of darkness,
   And bringeth forth the death-shade to the light of day.
23 He increaseth nations, and destroyeth them;
   He enlargeth nations, and carrieth them away.
24 He taketh away understanding from the chiefs of the people of the earth,
   And causeth them to wander in a pathless desert.
25 They grope in darkness, and there is no light,
   Yea, He maketh them to reel like a drunken man.

CHAPTER XIII.

1 Lo! all this hath mine eye seen,
  Mine ear hath heard, and discerned it for itself.
2 Whatsoever ye know, I myself know also;
  In no respect do I fall beneath you.
3 Surely I would commune with the Almighty,
  And I earnestly desire to plead my cause with God.
4 For verily ye are forgers of lies,
  Fabricators of nothingness all of you.
5 O that ye would be altogether silent,
  This indeed would be your wisdom.
6 Hear ye now my arguing,
  Yea, hearken to the pleadings of my lips.

7 Will ye speak iniquitously on God's behalf?
　Yea, on His behalf will ye utter fallacies?
8 Will ye act with partiality
　When ye contend on God's behalf?
9 Would it be well for you, that He should thoroughly search you out?
　Or can ye deceive Him as man is deceived?
10 Thoroughly He will chastise you,
　If secretly ye act with partiality.
11 Shall not His Majesty dismay you?
　And the dread of Him fall upon you?
12 Your aphorisms are parables of ashes,
　Your (sententious) collections, collections of mire.
13 Be silent and cease from me, and I will speak,
　Myself (will speak), then come on me whatever may.
14 Come what may, *I will take my flesh in my teeth*,
　And put my life in my hands.
15 Though He slay me, yet will I trust in Him,
　But I will vindicate my ways before Him.
16 He also shall be my salvation,
　For none profane shall come into His presence.
17 Hearken diligently to my words,
　And to my declaration with your ears.
18 Behold, now I have set my cause in order,
　I know that I shall be justified.
19 Who is he that will plead against me?
　Verily should I now be silent, I should expire.
20 But, O God, do two things on my behalf,
　Then will I not hide myself from Thy presence.
21 Remove Thy hand from off me,
　　And let not the dread of Thee dismay me.
22 Then summon Thou, and I myself will answer,
　Or I will speak, and reply Thou to me.

23 How many are mine iniquities, and my sins?
   Make me to know my transgression and my sin.
24 Wherefore hidest Thou Thy face,
   And accountest me Thine enemy?
25 Wilt Thou crush the driven leaf?
   And wilt Thou pursue the parched stubble?
26 Behold, Thou writest bitter things against me,
   And makest me to inherit the sins of my youth.
27 Yea, Thou placest my feet in fetters,
   And Thou watchfully eyest all my ways:
   To the soles of my feet Thou circumscribest bounds.

28 Lo, he dissolveth as rottenness,
   As a garment which the moth-worm consumeth,

CHAPTER XIV.

1 Even man that is born of woman,
  Few of days and full of trouble.
2 Like a flower he bloometh and is cut down,
  Yea, like a shadow he flitteth away, and abideth not.
3 Even upon such an one openest Thou Thine eyes,
  And bringest me into judgment with Thee.
4 Who can bring forth one that is pure?
  Free from pollution there is none.
5 Surely his days are determined,
  The number of his months is with Thee;
  Thou hast appointed his bound, which he cannot pass.
6 Turn away Thine eyes from him, that he may rest
  Until he as an hireling shall have fulfilled his day.
7 There is indeed hope for a tree
  That, if it be cut down, it will shoot forth again,
  And that its sprout will not fail.

8 Though its root shall have grown old in the earth,
  And its stump shall have become dead above ground.
9 From the inhaling of water it will again germinate,
  And put forth boughs like a sapling.
10 But man dieth, and is laid in the earth,
  Yea, man expireth, and where is he?
11 The waters from the sea (Nile) fail,
  And the wady is exhausted and drieth up;
12 So man lieth down and ariseth not,
  Until the heavens be no more they shall not awake,
  Nor from their sleep shall they be aroused.
13 O that Thou wouldest secrete me in Sheol,
  That Thou wouldest hide me until Thy anger be turned away,
  That Thou wouldest decree for me, and remember me!
14 If a man die, himself shall live again;
  All the days of my warfare will I wait
  Till my renovation come.
15 Thou wilt call, and I will answer Thee;
  Thou wilt yearn over the work of Thine own hands.
16 Dost Thou not now number my footsteps?
  Dost Thou not watch over my sins?
17 My transgression is sealed up in a bag,
  Yea, Thou sewest up mine iniquity.
18 Truly as the falling mountain dissolveth,
  And the rock moulders away from its place,
19 As the waters wear away the stones,
  As their overflowings wash away the dust of the earth,
  So Thou destroyest the hope of man.
20 Thou dost overpower him for ever, and he departeth,
  Thou dost change his countenance, and sendest him away.
21 His descendants come to honour, and he knoweth it not,
  Or they are brought low, but he discerneth them not.
22 But whilst his flesh is upon him, it shall suffer pain,
  And whilst his life is in him, it shall mourn.

CHAP. XIII. VER. 23 to CHAP. XIV. VER. 22.—From xiii. 23 to the end of chapter xiv. Job addresses the Almighty. This whole address is most sublime and pathetic. This picture of man's brevity of life, of his predestined death, of the rest of his disembodied spirit in Sheol until his resurrection, and of Job's expectancy of renovation from the dust of death to the glories of eternity, is inimitable. It is the Patriarch's creed of man's futurity.

VER. 27. *In fetters.*—To the ordinary English reader the word rendered by some CLOG would be ambiguous, and possibly might convey an erroneous idea. STOCKS, the rendering of the Authorized Version, is the version of another Hebrew noun, and seems less suitable to this verse than the more general term FETTERS.

CHAP. XIV. VER. 11. *The sea.*—The Nile is called the sea (*Isaiah* xix. 5, xxvii. 1 ; *Nahum* iii. 8). And in Job xli. 31 the word SEA signifies a RIVER rather than the ocean properly so called. The meaning of this verse is -As the Nile, which generally overflows the greater part of Egypt, recedes from the land, and floods the country no more, until at the return of the year it shall again inundate and fertilize the soil—as the wadys by the heat of summer are dried up and disappear, until the rains of winter shall replenish and fill with torrents of water their dry water-courses, so none of the souls of men shall be evoked from Sheol, and none of the bodies of men shall be raised from their graves, and none shall re-appear upon the earth, until the first resurrection of the saints to glory, and the establishment of Christ's millennial kingdom upon earth.

VER. 12. *Until the heavens be no more.*—Every man will be raised in his own order. There will be two resurrections, one resurrection of the saved at the beginning of Christ's millennial kingdom on earth, and one resurrection of the lost at the end of His millennial reign. The first resurrection will be preceded by the displacement of the FIGURATIVE heavens and luminaries. "Lo! there was a great earthquake, and the sun became black as sackcloth of hair, and the moon became as blood, and the stars of heaven fell unto the earth, even as a fig-tree casteth her untimely figs, when she is shaken of a mighty wind ; and the heaven departed as a scroll when it is rolled together, and every mountain and island were moved out of their places ; and the kings of the earth, and the great men, and the rich men, and the chief captains, and the mighty men, and every bondman, and every freeman, hid themselves in the dens and in the rocks of the mountains, and said to the mountains and rocks, Fall on us, and hide us from the face of Him that sitteth on the throne, and from the wrath of the Lamb, for the great day of His wrath is come, and who shall be able to stand?" (*Revelation* vi. 12-17). "And all the host of heaven shall be dissolved, and the heavens shall be rolled together as a scroll, and all their host shall fall down, as the leaf falleth off from the vine, and as a falling fig from the fig-tree" (*Isaiah* xxxiv. 4). The second resurrection and the final day of universal judgment will be preceded by the passing away of the existing LITERAL heavens and earth. "And I saw a great white throne, and Him that sat on it, from whose face the earth and the heaven fled away, and there was found no place for them" (*Revelation* xx. 12). "And I saw a new heaven and a new earth, for the first heaven and the first earth were passed away" (*Revelation* xxi. 1). Thus accurate is the predictive phraseology of Scripture. The righteous dead will not be raised from the dust and corruption of the grave, until the FIGURATIVE heavens, and their FIGURATIVE luminaries, the potentates of the Roman earth, shall be no more. The unbelieving dead will not be raised until the literal, that is the SIDEREAL heavens now existing shall have passed away, and be no more, to be succeeded by a new heaven and a new earth, and by the holy city, new Jerusalem, coming down from God out of heaven, prepared as a bride adorned for her husband. The resurrection of the righteous will immediately precede Christ's kingdom upon earth, when they shall be made Kings and Priests, and reign with Christ on earth 1000 years (*Revelation* i. 6, v. 10, xx. 4-6). The resurrection of the ungodly will immediately precede the final judgment of quick and dead and the celestial and sempiternal glory of the saints.

VER. 14. *My renovation.*—The word rendered in our version CHANGE, and by me RENOVATION, does not signify our being unclothed, but our being "clothed upon with our house which is from heaven, that mortality might be swallowed up of life" (2 *Corinthians* v. 2-4) –not the deposit of our corruptible bodies in the grave, but our being clothed with incorruption and immortality. "This corruptible must put on incorruption, and this mortal must put on immortality. So when this corruptible shall have put on incorruption, and this mortal shall have put on immortality, then shall be brought to pass the saying that is written, Death is swallowed up in victory" (1 *Corinthians* xv. 53, 54). The rendering of the LXX. accords with this interpretation : ἕως πάλιν γένωμαι, "till I am made again, or anew."---See *Parkhurst's Hebrew Lexicon.*

SECOND SPEECH OF ELIPHAZ THE TEMANITE.

CHAPTER XV.

Eliphaz censures Job, because he had justified himself, although by his own confession he had sinned against God.

Eliphaz affirms from his own experience, and from tradition (apparently the traditions of those saved in the Ark, arbitrarily arranged, and groundlessly applied to the case of Job), that sin against God is ALWAYS *punished by secular infliction upon the transgressor, and upon his posterity.*

1 Then responded Eliphaz the Temanite, and said :

2 Should a wise man answer with windy knowledge?
   And swell his bosom with the east wind ?

3 Shall he argue with speech which profits not?
   Or with words wherein there is no benefit ?

4 Yea, thou thyself dost cast off reverence,
   And withholdest prayer before God.

5 For thine own mouth proclaimeth thine iniquity,
   Though thou hast made choice of the tongue of the crafty ;

6 Thine own mouth condemneth thee, and not I,
   Yea, thine own lips testify against thee.

7 Art thou the first man born ?
   Yea, wast thou begotten before the hills ?

8 Hast thou listened to the secret council of God ?
   And hast thou from thence derived knowledge to thyself ?

9 What knowest thou that we know not ?
   What dost thou understand with which we are not conversant ?

10 Among us are both the hoary-headed and the very aged,
   In days surpassing thy father.

11 Are the consolations of God of little account with thee ?
   And the word which deals so gently with thee ?

12 Whither doth thine heart bear thee away ?
   And upon what are thine eyes intensely fixed ?

13 That thou ventest thy spirit against God?
   And hast uttered taunts from thy mouth?
14 What is man, that he should be pure?
   And the offspring of woman, that he should be righteous?
15 Behold, He confideth not in His holy ones,
   Yea, the heavens are unclean in His sight.
16 Surely then abominable and corrupt is man,
   Who drinketh in iniquity as water.
17 I will show thee, hearken thou to me,
   And that which I have seen I will declare.
18 That which wise men have related,
   And which they have not concealed (having received it) from their fathers.
19 To whom, to whom alone, the earth was given,
   And among whom no stranger passed.
20 All the days of the wicked one, he is his own tormentor,
   And a reckoning of years is laid up for the oppressor.
21 Fearful sounds are in his ears,
   In his security the destroyer cometh upon him.
22 He hath no assurance, that he shall return out of darkness,
   But (believeth) that he is marked out for the sword.
23 He is a wanderer. As for bread, where is it?
   He knows that the day of darkness is ready at his very hand.
24 Distress and anguish dismay him,
   As a king ready for battle they overpower him.
25 Because he stretched forth his hand against God,
   And proudly exalted himself against the Almighty.
26 (Because) he rushed against Him with outstretched neck,
   With the thick bosses of his bucklers.
27 Because he enveloped his face in fatness,
   And heaped fat upon his loins.
28 Therefore in desolate cities he shall dwell,
   In houses which no man inhabiteth,
   Which are ready to become ruinous heaps.

29 He shall not grow rich, nor shall his wealth endure,
Nor shall their prosperity be extended over the land.

30 He shall not escape out of darkness,
The lightning shall wither his branches,
And by the blast of His mouth shall he be taken away.

31 Let not him that is deceived trust in evil,
For evil shall be his recompense.

32 (His recompense) shall be consummated before his day is accomplished,
And his branch shall not flourish.

33 He shall shed his unripe grapes like the vine,
And shall cast off his blossoms like the olive.

34 For the clan of the profane shall be a barren rock,
And fire shall consume the tents of corruption,

35 Conceiving mischief, and bringing forth iniquity,
Yea, their womb matures deceit.

CHAP. XV. VER. 10. *The hoary-headed and the very aged.*—By these words Eliphaz refers most evidently to Noah, Shem, Ham, Japhet, and to Eber, who attained to a greater longevity than any other patriarch born after the flood, having died at the age of 464. Noah, Shem, and Eber were undoubtedly living at the era of Job's temptation, and when Eliphaz was then arguing. It is most highly probable that Japhet and Ham were then alive. I understand Noah, Shem, Ham, Japhet, and Eber to be the very " hoary-headed and the very aged, surpassing the age of Job's father," especially alluded to in this verse. See Matthew Henry's Chrono-Genealogical Chart of the Second Age of the World, or the Post-Diluvian Patriarchs from the Deluge to the Call of Abraham, in the seventh volume of his works by Burder and Hughes.

VERS. 19. *To whom alone the earth was given.*—I know not of whom by any possibility these words could have been spoken by Eliphaz, but of Noah and the inmates of the ark. Noah was the second universal father of the human race. From him, as well as from Adam, all the post-diluvian generations of men have descended. When Noah and his family came forth from the ark, they were the sole inheritors and possessors of this terraqueous globe. The dominion of the earth, originally granted to Adam and the Adamic race, was transferred to Noah, Shem, Ham, and Japhet.

" To whom, to whom alone, the earth was given,
And among whom no stranger passed."

The tenth chapter of Genesis is an ethnographical delineation of the settlements of the three sons of Noah, and of the partition of the five quarters of the world among them, its sole and exclusive possessors. "These are the families of the sons of Noah, after their generations, in their nations; and by these were the nations divided in the earth after the flood" (x. 32).

The proverbial sayings of this chapter from verse 20 to 35, were the patriarchal maxims of Shem, Ham, and Japhet, and of their descendants previous to the age of Peleg (in whose time the earth was divided among the posterity of Noah), as handed down by tradition, and received by Eliphaz. That WHATEVER A MAN SOWETH THAT SHALL HE ALSO REAP is a truism, which none can contradict. But that the punition of sin is ALWAYS inflicted in time, either upon the transgressor or upon his posterity, and NEVER reserved for eternity; and that suffering in time is ALWAYS the result and punishment of sin committed, is a deduction from this premise, which has no warrant in Scripture, and which these patriarchal proverbs, arbitrarily arranged, and improperly applied to the case of Job, cannot justify.

REPLY OF JOB TO THE SECOND SPEECH OF ELIPHAZ.

CHAPTERS XVI. AND XVII.

Job ascribeth to God the bitterness of his affliction, resulting from God's mysterious permission to Satan to buffet him and bring him near the dust of death. The Patriarch vindicates his own innocency, as contrasted with his fellow-men, and asserts his faith in the predicted Intercessor, the promised Seed of the woman, who as his friend should mediate with God for him. He denounceth the embittered argumentation of his friends, and their want of sympathy for him in his sufferings and proximity to death.

1 Then responded Job, and said :

2 Innumerable sayings like these have I heard :
   Miserable comforters are ye all.

3 Will there be an end to words of wind ?
   Yea, what hath emboldened thee, that thou shouldest answer me thus ?

4 I myself also could speak as ye do,
   If ye were now in my place.

   I could string together words against you,
   And could shake my head at you.

5 With my own mouth could I overpower you,
   Until the motion of my lips should fail.

6 If I speak, my grief is not assuaged,
   And if I desist, how does it depart from me ?

7 For now He hath outwearied me,
   All my household Thou hast brought to desolation.

8 And Thou hast enchained me, and this witnesses against me,
   Yea, my wasting away rises up against me, it testifies to my face.

9 His anger preyeth upon (me) and persecutes me,
   He gnasheth upon me with his teeth,
   Mine adversary sharpeneth his eyes against me.

F

10 They gape upon me with their mouth,
   In scorn they smite my cheeks,
   They have conspired together against me.

11 God hath delivered me up to the Evil One,
   And hath cast me down by the hands of wicked men.

12 I was at rest, but He hath broken me up,
   He hath also seized me by the neck, and shaken me to pieces,
   Yea, He hath set me up to be His mark.

13 His arrows beset me round about,
   He transfixed my reins, and spared not,
   My life-gall He hath poured upon the ground

14 He stormeth me with breach upon breach,
   He rusheth upon me like a mighty warrior.

15 Sackcloth have I sewed together upon my skin,
   And I have rolled my turban in the dust.

16 My face is reddened with weeping,
   And death-shade is upon my eyelids ;

17 Though there hath been no injustice in my hands,
   And my prayer has been pure.

18 O earth, cover no blood shed by me,
   And be there no hiding-place for cries against me.

19 Behold also now my witness is in heaven,
   And my eyewitness is in the highest.

20 My Mediator is my friend ;
   Mine eye weeps unto God.

21 And He (the Mediator) will plead with God for man,
   Yea, the Son of Man (will plead) for His friend.

22 When the years numbered to me shall have come,
   Then shall I go the way from whence I shall not return.

CHAPTER XVII.

1 My breath is oppressed,
My days are extinct,
The grave is my portion.

2 Are not mockers present with me?
And doth not mine eye rest on their embitterings?

3 Appoint now my surety with Thee;
Who is he that will strike hands with me?

4 Behold, Thou hast kept back their heart from understanding,
Therefore Thou wilt not exalt them.

5 He who discloseth his friends for a prey,
The eyes of his children shall waste away.

6 And me hath He set as a byeword among the nations;
I am become one to be spit upon in the face.

7 Mine eye also is bedimmed with sorrow,
And my limbs, all of them, are like a shadow.

8 The upright will be confounded at this,
And the innocent will rouse himself against the profane.

9 The righteous shall hold on his way,
And he that hath clean hands shall wax stronger and stronger.

10 But as for you all, get you hence and be gone, I pray,
For I cannot find among you one wise man.

11 My days are past, my projects are broken off,
The cherished prepossessions of my heart.

12 My night is changed into day,
Into light bordering on darkness.

13 Lo! I await Sheol to be my home,
I have spread my bed in the darkness.

14 I have called to corruption, "Thou art my father;"
And to the worm, "My mother, my sister!"

15 And in such a state, where are my hopes?
Yea, my hopes, who regardeth them?

16 To the depths of Sheol Thou makest them to descend,
Verily to the dust shall all descend together.

CHAP. XVI. VER. 10. *They gape upon me with their mouth.*—A striking similarity exists between the diction of this verse and of iv. 8, 9, and xix. 13, 19, and the inspired language of David and St. Paul.

Job xvi. 10 —They gape upon me with their mouth.
Psalm xxii. 13. They gaped upon me with their mouths.
Job xix. 13-15, 19.—My brethren He hath removed far from me,
 And they that know me are wholly estranged from me.
 My kinsfolk have deserted me,
 And they that know me have forgotten me.
 I am become an alien in their sight.
 All my familiar friends have abhorred me,
 And they whom I have loved have turned against me.
Psalm xxxviii. 11.—My lovers and My friends stand aloof from My sore,
 And My kinsmen stand afar off.
Psalm lxix. 8. I am become a stranger unto My brethren,
 And an alien to My mother's children.
Psalm lxxxviii. 8, 18. Thou hast put away Mine acquaintance far from Me,
 Thou hast made Me an abomination unto them:
 Lover and friend hast Thou put far from me,
 And mine acquaintance into darkness.
Job iv. 8, 9.- The ploughers of iniquity,
 And the sowers of wickedness, reap the same.
 By the blast of God they perish,
 And by the breath of His nostrils they are consumed.

2 Thessalonians ii. 8. Then shall that wicked be revealed, whom the Lord (Jesus) shall consume with the spirit of His mouth, and shall destroy with the brightness of His coming.

If the words of David and St. Paul are not quotations from the Poem of Job, they at least have an allusive reference thereto. May we not deduce therefrom, that the same malign, diabolic influence instigated the ungodly Idumæan Arabs to deride and mock Job amidst his sufferings, which instigated the Jewish multitude to exclaim: "Not this man, but Barabbas —Crucify Him! Crucify Him! -He saved others, Himself He cannot save His blood be on us and on our children!"—and that the same intervention of Satan caused the desertion of Job by his wife, relatives, and friends, which caused the desertion of Christ by the multitudes He had healed, by His brethren, and by the Apostles whom he had chosen? May we not deduce therefrom, that the language of Eliphaz foreshadows the retributive justice to be visited upon "the man of sin and son of perdition," the Antichrist of prophecy: "Reward her (Babylon the great) even as she rewarded you, and double unto her double, according to her works: in the cup which she hath filled, fill to her double?"—*Revelation* xviii. 6.

VER. 11.—The language of Job in this verse clearly evidences his correct conception of the origin and instrumentality of his afflictive spoliation, bereavement, and excruciating disease. He recognises the sovereignty of God in delivering him for gracious but unseen purposes into the power of Satan, who otherwise would have been powerless to injure him. He recounts the malignant influence of the evil Spirit operating on the hearts of the unregenerate, and employing them as his instruments to afflict him. He announces his decided conviction, that it was Satan who instigated the Sabæans and Chaldæans to despoil him of his cattle, and who employed lightning to destroy his sheep, and the fell simoom wind to kill his sons and daughters. Satan is yet the God of this world, and the Prince of the power of the air, seeking whom he may devour. This world is the devil's world, as far as permission from on high is mysteriously conceded to the Evil Spirit. He yet "wanders to and fro in the earth, and walks up and down in it." What need have we then to pray, as Christ himself hath taught us. "Lead us not into temptation, but deliver us from the Evil One."

VER 20. *Mine eye weeps unto God.*—" With silent flow
 Mine eye, to God, reveals my bitter woe."—*Stather.*

These words express Job's repentance towards God combined with faith in the promised Messiah, Job's contrition for sin committed, combined with assurance of remission and salvation.

CHAP. XVII. VER. 3. *Strike hands with me.*—"To strike hands with another is a general and well-known emblem of AGREEMENT, BARGAINING, or SURETYSHIP."—Parkhurst's *Hebrew Lexicon.*

SECOND SPEECH OF BILDAD THE SHUHITE.

CHAPTER XVIII.

Bildad reproves Job, and with caustic severity reiterates the fallacy, that suffering in this present life is the necessary inseparable consequent and punishment of sin committed.

1 Then responded Bildad the Shuhite, and said:

2 How long will ye plant thorns among words?
 Understand us, and afterwards we will speak.

3 Why are we accounted as brutes?
 Why are we become vile in your sight?

4 Destroyer of himself in his fury!
 Must the earth be deserted for thee?
 And the rock be removed from its place?

5 Behold, the light of the wicked shall be extinguished,
 And the flame of his fire shall blaze no more.

6 Daylight in his tent shall be darkness,
 And his lamp over him shall be extinguished.

7 His mighty strides shall be straitened,
 And his own counsel shall cast him down.

8 For he is brought into the net by his own feet,
 And he directeth his steps over the pitfall.

9 The snare shall seize him by the heel,
 And the gin shall take fast hold of him.

10 A noose to catch him is latent in the ground,
 And a trap is laid for him in the pathway.

11 Terrors alarm him on every side,
 And confound him even to his footsteps.

12 Hunger-bitten shall be his strength,
 And destruction shall be present at his side.

13 Gluttonously shall it feed on his skin,
 The first-born of death shall feed on him gluttonously.

14 He shall be uprooted from his tent, his confidence,
 And dissolution like a king shall march against him.

15 It (dissolution) shall dwell in his tent, no longer his;
   Brimstone shall be showered upon his habitation.
16 His roots below shall be burned up,
   And above his branch shall be cut off.
17 His memory perisheth from the earth,
   And he shall have no name in the street.
18 He shall be thrust forth from light into darkness,
   And shall be chased from the habitable world.
19 He shall have neither son nor progeny among his people,
   Nor any survivor in his dwellings.
20 After-generations shall be astonished at his day,
   As former-generations were horror-stricken.
21 Surely such are the dwellings of the impious man,
   And such is the habitation of him who acknowledgeth not God.

CHAP. XVIII. VERS. 12, 13.—In these two verses Bildad most cruelly depicts, in Oriental poetic diction, that loathsome ulceration with which the body of Job was afflicted. He calls it DESTRUCTION, because the elephantiasis was incurable by medical skill. He represents it feeding on THE SKIN, because the elephantiasis is a skin complaint; first of all affecting the skin, and afterwards affecting the flesh, the muscles, the bones, the whole of the human frame. He designates it the FIRST-BORN OF DEATH, because it was pre-eminently the most fatal of all diseases known in North-Western Arabia. As primogeniture gave to the first-born pre-eminence of rank and property, so the elephantiasis was pre-eminent above all other known diseases in inflicting severity of suffering and certainty of death. See description of the elephantiasis in note on ii. 7.

REPLY OF JOB TO THE SECOND SPEECH OF BILDAD.

CHAPTER XIX.

Job attributeth unto God his misery, and his desertion by his wife, his brethren, his acquaintance, and his servants, and imploreth the compassion of his three friends.

Job asserteth his faith in his Redeemer, who is, and was, and is to come, the Almighty, and in his own glorious resurrection from the dust of death, and in his vindication from the aspersions of his three friends on the day of judgment, when the books shall be opened, and the dead shall be judged out of the things written in the books, and God will render to every man according to his works.

1 Then responded Job, and said:

2 How long will ye vex my soul,
   And crush me with words?

3 These ten times have ye reviled me,
   Ye are not ashamed, though ye have known me well.
4 And have I indeed erred?
   My error remaineth with myself.
5 If indeed ye will magnify yourselves against me,
   Then prove against me my reproach.
6 Know now that God hath overthrown me,
   And hath encompassed me with His toils.
7 Behold, I cry out because of violence, but am not answered,
   I call aloud, but there is no justice.
8 He hath hedged up my way, so that I cannot go forward,
   And upon my paths hath He cast darkness.
9 My glory hath He stripped from off me,
   And the crown hath He removed from my head.
10 He destroys me on every side, and I perish,
   And He uprooteth my hope as a tree.
11 Yea, He kindleth His fury against me,
   And accounteth me to be unto Him as one of His enemies.
12 His troops advance together,
   And cast up their lines against me;
   They encamp round about my tent.
13 My brethren He hath removed far from me,
   And they that know me are wholly estranged from me.
14 My kinsfolk have deserted me,
   And they that know me have forgotten me.
15 The dwellers in my house, even my own maid-servants,
   Count me as a stranger;
   I have become an alien in their sight.
16 I called to my man-servant, and he gave me no answer;
   With my own mouth did I entreat him.
17 My life is loathsome to my wife,
   And my entreaties to the children of the womb which bare me.

18 Even the young children spurn at me,
   I rise up, and they speak against me.

19 All my familiar friends have abhorred me,
   And they whom I have loved have turned against me.

20 My bones cleave to my skin and to my flesh,
   And that which my teeth have eaten, I eject.

21 Have pity upon me, have pity upon me, O ye my friends,
   For the hand of God hath smitten me.

22 Why, as if ye were God, do ye persecute me?
   And why are ye not satisfied with my flesh?

23 Oh that my words were now written down!
   Oh that they were engraven upon a tablet!

24 That with an iron graver and with lead
   They were sculptured upon a rock for ever!

25 Verily I know my Redeemer is THE LIVING ONE,
   And He, THE LAST, shall o'er the dust ascend:

26 And after disease shall have destroyed my skin,
   That apart from my flesh shall I see God,

27 Whom I shall see mine own,
   And mine eyes shall behold Him, yea, not estranged,
   Though my reins shall have been consumed within me.

28 Then shall ye say, How did we persecute him?
   When the root of the matter shall have been found in me.

29 O tremble for yourselves before the sword,
   For (your) fiery heat is a crime for the sword to punish,
   That ye may indeed understand that there is a judgment to come.

CHAP. XIX. VERS. 13-15 and 19.—See note on xvi. 10.

VER. 17. *Children of the womb which bare me*, that is, MY BROTHERS AND SISTERS. These are mentioned, xlii. 11:
"Then came unto him all his brethren,
And all his sisters."

VER. 20.—The adhesion of the bones to the cuticle of the outer skin, and their consequent apparent prominence, evidence the greatness of the emaciation of Job. This emaciation would be greatly increased and continued by his stomach rejecting food. The rendering of the second line of this verse is substantially that of Fry, which see. This rendering makes clear and intelligible what hitherto has been acknowledged to have been abstruse and difficult—a *crux interpretum*. The Hebrew verb in Hithpael occurs in Job xli. 19 (11) in the same acceptation as in this verse.

VER. 22. *Why are ye not satisfied with my flesh?*—"Why are you not, like God, satisfied with the destruction of my flesh, which you see is fast being accomplished? The chastisements of Eloah, my covenant-God, the Author of eternal life to me, can go no further, in virtue of His engagements. Where, therefore, you see God Himself finishing His infliction, why would you go further, and indulge your own maliciousness; and, when I should be the object of your pity, still keep pursuing me with your invectives, and grieving my soul with the most cruel accusations."—*Fry.*

VER. 23.—"Job's words have not been written with an iron style, as he had desired, but far more durably. Had they been written as he wished, time would have obliterated them, but they have been written in the imperishable records of Holy Scripture. They are graven on the rock of God's Word, and there are read, and minister comfort to all generations."—*Chrysostom.*

VER. 23-27.—I subjoin Scott's felicitous poetic version of this evangelical prophecy:—

"O that, fair written in a faithful scroll,
Time in his archives would my words enroll!
O furrow them in lead; their letters give
Through endless ages in the rock to live.
I know, that He whose years can ne'er decay
Will from the grave redeem my sleeping clay.
When the last rolling sun shall leave the skies,
He will survive, and o'er the dust arise:
Then shall this mangled skin NEW form assume,
This flesh then flourish in immortal bloom:
My raptured eyes the judging God shall see,
Estranged no more, but friendly then to me.
How does the lofty hope my soul inspire!
I burn, I faint with vehement desire."

VER. 25. *My Redeemer.*—"Goel, a near kinsman, one who by the Mosaic law had a right to REDEEM an inheritance, and also was permitted to VINDICATE or AVENGE the death of his relation by killing the slayer, if he found him out of the cities of refuge (see Numbers xxxv. 19, 21, etc.), and so was a type of Him who was to REDEEM man from death and the grave, to RECOVER for him the eternal inheritance, and to AVENGE HIM on Satan, his spiritual enemy and murderer. See Job xix. 25."—*Parkhurst's Hebrew Lexicon.*

VER. 25. THE LAST.—THE LAST is one of the names of the triune Jehovah, Father, Son, and Holy Spirit (*Isaiah* xli. 4, xliii. 10, xliv. 6, xlviii. 12); and in the Apocalypse is specially predicated of Christ (*Revelation* i. 8, 11, 17, ii. 8, xxi. 6, xxii. 13).

VER. 25. *Dust.*—Both the dust of the earth and the dust of the human race. "Out of the ground wast thou taken, for dust thou art, and unto dust shalt thou return" (*Genesis* iii. 19). "The Lord God formed man of the dust of the ground" (*Genesis* ii. 7).

VER. 26. *Apart from my flesh.*—"Flesh and blood cannot inherit the kingdom of God, neither doth corruption inherit incorruption—for this corruptible must put on incorruption, and this mortal must put on immortality" (1 *Corinthians* xv. 50 and 53). The bodies of the saints, created out of the dust of the ground, by death return to the original element of dust, whence they were formed. At the resurrection these original elements will be newly created in all things essential to their identity, without spot or wrinkle or other defilement, and with perfection of glory, reunion, and recognition, will be raised up after Christ's likeness. Then the risen saints, perfectly sanctified in body, soul, and spirit, shall see as they are seen, and know as they are known.—*See Conybeare and Howson on* 1 *Cor.* xv. 50.

"Flesh and blood
Inherit not that kingdom. Ashes, dust,
Unto the dust return. Consuming fire,
All that is earthly, burneth. We must bear
Another image, heavenly— put on
A spiritual body without sin
Of other blood compacted: flesh of flesh,
Bone of that bone in virgin womb conceived
When overshadow'd of the Holy Ghost
A nature without spot, divine, more pure
Than Adam's in his innocence."—*Palingenesia,* by Lewis Way.

VER. 27. *Mine own.*—"This God is MY God for ever and ever. He will be MY guide unto death."—*Psalm* xlviii. 14.

SECOND SPEECH OF ZOPHAR THE NAAMATHITE.

CHAPTER XX.

Zophar, with bitter acrimony, reiterates the fallacy that sin is ALWAYS *visited by punishment in this present life, and that in man's time-state here below suffering is the inevitable and certain consequent of sin committed.*

1 Then responded Zophar the Naamathite, and said :

2 Truly tumultuous thoughts compel me to reply,
   Yea, on account of the impetuous ardour within me.

3 I have heard thy ignominious reproof of me,
   And the spirit of my understanding constrains me to answer.

4 Hast thou not known this to have existed of old,
   From the time that man was placed upon the earth,

5 That short-lived is the jubilation of the wicked,
   And momentary is the rejoicing of the profane ?

6 Though his exaltation should mount up to the heavens,
   And his head should reach the clouds,

7 Yet like his own dung shall he utterly perish,
   They who have seen him shall say, " Where is he ? "

8 As a dream he shall flit away, and shall not be found,
   Yea, he shall vanish as a vision of the night.

9 The eye which saw him shall see him no more,
   And his place shall never more behold him.

10 His children shall wander about beggars,
   Yea, his own hands shall make restitution of his wealth.

11 His bones are filled with the sins of his youth,
   Which shall lie down with him in the dust.

12 Though wickedness be sweet in his mouth,
   Though he hide it under his tongue,

13 Though he retain it and will not relinquish it,
   And though he hold it in his palate,

14 His food shall be changed in his intestines,
   And shall become the gall of asps within him.

15 He hath swallowed down wealth, but shall disgorge it,
   God shall dispossess his stomach of it.
16 He shall suck the poison of asps,
   The viper's tongue shall slay him.
17 He shall never look upon the rivulets,
   The valley-streams of honey and butter.
18 The produce of his labour he shall restore, and not consume,
   His restitution shall be proportionate to his wealth, which he shall not enjoy.
19 Because he hath crushed, and then abandoned the poor,
   Hath taken a house by violence which he hath not built,
20 Surely he shall not experience internal peace,
   He shall not save that in which he delighted.
21 Not a fragment shall remain for his food,
   For nought is the product of his prosperity.
22 In the fulness of his abundance he shall be distressed,
   Every branch of misery shall come upon him.
23 It shall be while he is filling his belly,
   That (God) shall cast down upon him the fierceness of His wrath,
   And shall rain it upon him while he is eating.
24 If he fly from the iron weapon,
   The brazen bow shall pierce him through,
25 He plucks out (the arrow) and it comes forth from his body,
   Yea, the gleaming weapon from his gall,
   Terrors shall come upon him.
26 Every horror is treasured up in store for him,
   A fire not blown shall consume him,
   It shall devour the remnant in his tent.
27 The heavens shall unveil his iniquity,
   And the earth shall rise up against him.
28 The substance of his house shall be carried away,
   And shall be a rack in the day of His wrath—
29 Such is the lot of the wicked man from God,
   And the heritage ordained by God unto him.

CHAP. XX. VER. 16. *Asps.*—"The Hebrew word occurs six times. It evidently denotes some poisonous serpent, that dwells in holes, that the serpent-charmers were in the habit of exercising upon, probably the Egyptian Cobra (*naja haje*), well known in Southern Palestine."—Tristram's *Natural History.*

VER. 16. *Viper's tongue.*—"The Hebrew word occurs three times. I have identified it with the *echis arenicola*, or Sand Viper, a species of small size, about a foot long, varying in colour, and very common through the whole of the sandy regions of North Africa from West to East, and in Arabia and Syria. We found it frequently in winter, under stones, by the shores of the Dead Sea. It is very rapid and active in its movements. Though highly poisonous, it is not so much to be dreaded as the fatal Cobra or Cerastes."—Tristram's *Natural History.*

VER. 17. *The rivulets, the valley-streams.*—The Authorized Version, THE RIVERS, cannot be correct, as there are no rivers in Arabia, and only the Jordan in Palestine. Arabia is watered and fertilized by wadys or winter-torrents, generally dry in summer, but roaring with water in the winter months. The valley-streams here mentioned are synonymous with wadys, so abundant in Arabia and Palestine. The Hebrew word may indifferently signify RIVERS or STREAMS. Its association with VALLEYS in this verse restricts its meaning to STREAMS in this passage.

REPLY OF JOB TO THE SECOND SPEECH OF ZOPHAR.

CHAPTER XXI.

Job refutes the arguments of his three friends by showing—
1. *That the wicked are in this life frequently prosperous in their persons and their families.*
2. *That the retributive justice of God frequently overtakes and punishes the wicked even in their time-state here below.*
3. *That some men enjoy uninterrupted prosperity.*
4. *That other men endure bitterness of soul and continued adversity.*
5. *That therefore there must be a Day of Judgment to come, when God will vindicate His ways with man, and will demonstrate to the assembled universe that He hath done, and doeth, all things well.*

1 Then responded Job, and said :

2 Listen attentively to my words,
And be this your condolence with me.

3 Bear with me, and I myself will speak,
And after that I have spoken, mock on !

4 As to myself, is my complaint addressed to man ?
And if so, why should not my spirit be vexed ?

5 Look upon me, and be astonished,
And lay (your) hand upon (your) mouth.

6 When indeed I have remembered, I have been confounded,
And horror hath seized my flesh.

7 Wherefore do the wicked live,
 Grow old, and even become mighty in wealth?

8 Their seed is established,
 Their family is present with them,
 And their offspring before their eyes.

9 Their houses are safe from alarms,
 And no scourge of God is upon them.

10 His bull gendereth, and refuseth not,
 His cow calveth, and casteth not her calf.

11 They send forth their little ones like a flock,
 And their children sportively dance.

12 They rise up to the timbrel and harp,
 And trip merrily to the sound of the pipe.

13 In prosperity they spend their days,
 And in a moment are brought down to Sheol.

14 Therefore they say unto God : " Depart from us,
 For we desire not the knowledge of Thy ways.

15 What is the Almighty that we should serve Him?
 And what will it profit us if we pray unto Him?"

16 Behold, their prosperity is not in their own keeping.
 Far be from me the advocacy of the wicked.

17 How often doth He extinguish the lamp of the wicked!
 And bring down their destruction upon them!
 How often doth He apportion tribulations in His anger!

18 How often are they as stubble before the wind!
 And as chaff which the whirlwind whirls away!

19 How often doth God treasure up for his sons the punishment due to himself!
 He requites it upon himself, and he knows it.

20 His own eyes see his entrapment,
 And he drinketh of the wrath of the Almighty.

21 Lo! how doth he punish him in his family after him!
   And cut short to him the number of his months!

22 Who shall impart knowledge to God?
   Seeing He shall judge him eaten up of worms?

23 One man dieth in his entire strength,
   Being wholly at ease and quiet.

24 His intestines are full of fat,
   And his bones are moist with marrow.

25 And another dieth in bitterness of soul,
   And hath never tasted of prosperity.

26 Together they lie down in the dust,
   And worms cover them.

27 Behold, I am cognisant of your devices,
   And of the machinations wherewith you would oppress me.

28 For ye say, " Where is the house of the noble?
   Where is the tent, the habitation of the wicked?"

29 Surely! thou canst never have inquired of men of travel,
   Or thou couldest not have been ignorant of their intimations,

30 That the wicked is preserved to the day of destruction,
   That they are prolonged for the day of great wrath.

31 Who denounceth his conduct to his face?
   And who requiteth him for what he hath done?

32 Yet shall he be borne in procession to the grave,
   And over his tomb watch shall be kept.

33 Sweetly rest on him the clods of the valley,
   And after him shall march all the people,
   And before him an innumerable multitude.

34 Why then offer ye to me vain condolences,
   Seeing that your answers are the leaven of deceit?

CHAP. XXI. VERS. 23-26.—" How various the circumstances of people's dying are! There is one way into the world, but many out; yet, as some are born by quick and easy labour, others by that which is hard and lingering, so dying is to some much more terrible than to others; and since the death of the body is the birth of the soul into another world, deathbed agonies may not unfitly be compared to childbed throes."—*Henry.*

THIRD SPEECH OF ELIPHAZ THE TEMANITE.

CHAPTER XXII.

Eliphaz imputes to Job harshness, severity, and oppression, and ascribes to these criminalities, with which he charges the patriarch, his present sufferings.

Eliphaz asserts the omnipotence and sovereignty of God in the administration of the universe, and exemplifies these perfections as specially manifested in the deluge of Divine wrath on the world of the ungodly.

Eliphaz promises to Job, on his repentance, contrition, and reformation, uninterrupted felicity in life and death, in body and soul, in time and in eternity.

1 Then responded Eliphaz the Temanite, and said:

2 Can a man profit God?
Verily it is himself the wise man profits.

3 Does it concern the Almighty that thou shouldest be righteous?
Or is it gain (to Him) that thou shouldest perfect thy ways?

4 Will He on account of thy piety plead with thee?
Will He enter into judgment with thee?

5 Has not thy wickedness been great?
And have not thine iniquities been infinite?

6 Verily thou hast taken a pledge from thy brethren for nought,
And hast stripped off the clothing of the desolate.

7 To the fainting thou hast given no water to drink,
And from the famishing thou hast withholden bread.

8 Thus the man of power possessed the land as his own,
And the honoured of men dwelleth therein.

9 Widows thou hast sent away empty,
And crushed have been the arms of the fatherless.

10 Therefore snares encompass thee on every side,
And consternation suddenly confounds thee,

11 And darkness, so that thou canst not see,
And inundations of waters cover thee.

12 Is not God high above the heavens?
   And does He not look down upon the topmost stars, however high
      they are?

13 Yet thou sayest, "How can God know?
   Can He judge through the dense darkness?

14 Thick clouds are a covering to Him that He cannot see,
   And He walketh upon the vault of heaven."

15 Hast thou marked the way of olden times,
   Which wicked men have trodden?

16 Who were prematurely cut off,
   The flood inundating their foundation:

17 Who said unto God: "Depart from us,
   And what can the Almighty do for them,

18 Though He hath filled their houses with good?"
   Far from me be the advocacy of the wicked.

19 The righteous see and rejoice,
   And the innocent hold them in derision, (saying)

20 "Truly was not (their) rising against us quelled?
   And did not wrath consume their abundance?"

21 Commune, I beseech thee, with Him, and have peace,
   Thereby shall good come upon thee.

22 Receive, I pray thee, the law from His mouth,
   And lay up His words in thy heart.

23 If thou return to the Almighty, thou shalt be built up;
   If thou put away iniquity from thy tents,

24 And shalt regard gold as dust,
   And Ophir-gold as the quartz of wadys,

25 Then shall the Almighty be thy precious ores,
   And shalt be to thee silver extracted with toil.

26 For then shalt thou delight thyself in the Almighty,
And shalt lift up thy face unto God.

27 Then thou shalt pray to Him, and He will hear thee,
And thou shalt fulfil thy vows.

28 Yea, thou shalt determine a thing, and it shall be accomplished by thee,
And light shall shine upon thy ways.

29 When men shall oppress, and thou shalt say, "Let there be exaltation,"
Then shall He save the man of lowly eyes.

30 The habitation of the innocent shall be delivered,
And shall be delivered through the pureness of thy hands.

CHAP. XXII. VER. 3. *Does it concern the Almighty.*—The Received Version of this line, "Is it any pleasure to the Almighty that thou art righteous?" cannot be correct. It is flatly contradictory to *Psalm* cxlvii. 11, "The Lord taketh pleasure in them that love Him;" to *Psalm* cxlix. 4, "The Lord taketh pleasure in them that fear Him;" to *Proverbs* xi. 20, "Such as are upright in their way are the delight of the Lord," etc. It is true that these are the words of Eliphaz, and not of Job. But we are not justified in imputing to either of the three friends of Job any erroneous sentiment which the original Hebrew of their speeches does not necessarily convey. The Hebrew word rendered in the Authorized Version PLEASURE admits of an acceptation accordant with the Divine will, and ought so to be rendered in this verse. The Genevan Version renders :—
 "Is it anything unto the Almightie, that thou art righteous?"
The Bishop's Bible renders :—
 "Is it any advantage to the Almightie, that thou art righteous?"
Rosenmüller subjoins this excellent note: "Nihil sane ex nostris operibus Deo accedat, qui absolutissimus quum sit, nullius iudiget."
VER. 17. *What can the Almighty do for them?*—What can the Almighty do for Noah and his family? How can God navigate the Ark, and insure preservation to its inmates? He hath indeed blessed them with secular prosperity. But how can He preserve them alive amidst the roaring billows of the predicted Deluge, and save them from that universal catastrophe, which they assert will annihilate all the posterity of Adam, the inmates of the Ark alone excepted?
VER. 20. *Wrath.*—The section of this chapter extending from verse 15 to verse 20 is a description of the impiety of the Antediluvians, of their rejection of the preaching and warnings of Noah, of their scoffs against the predicted Deluge, and of the entire destruction both of their persons and property. But we nowhere read of fire as an agent employed to effect the Deluge. Hence the Hebrew word more usually rendered FIRE is here translated WRATH. Lee in his Hebrew Lexicon gives it the meaning of FIERCE ANGER, Deuteronomy xxxii. 22, and Jeremiah xxi. 12. Rosenmüller in his note translates it, THE FIRE OF DIVINE WRATH, and, in vindication of this rendering, refers to Job xxxi. 12; Psalms xviii. 8, xxi. 9, lxxviii. 21. The parallelism of Psalm lxxviii. 21 fully warrants this signification :—
 "So a FIRE was kindled against Jacob,
 And ANGER also came up against Israel."
ANGER in the second hemistich defines the meaning of FIRE in the first hemistich.

H

REPLY OF JOB TO THE THIRD SPEECH OF ELIPHAZ.

CHAPTERS XXIII. AND XXIV.

Job, agonized by mental conflict, bodily sufferings, unfounded accusations, and the withdrawing of the Divine presence, earnestly desires that God would adjudicate his cause, and vindicate his integrity. He pleads not sinlessness, but sincerity and consistency of his faith and practice. He contrasts his own bitter sufferings with the secular prosperity of evil-doers, enumerates their criminalities against God and man, and bemoans the absence of Divine judgment on these children of the wicked one.

1 Then responded Job, and said:

2 Although bitter is my present complaining,
 The hand which is upon me is heavier than my lamentation.

3 Oh that I had knowledge where I could find Him,
 That I could come before His judgment-seat!

4 I would lay in order my cause before Him,
 And would fill my mouth with arguments;

5 I would know the words wherewith He would answer me,
 And understand what He would say unto me.

6 Would He contend with me in the mightiness of His power?
 No! Surely He would set His heart upon me.

7 Then the upright might plead with Him,
 And I should victoriously be absolved from my condemnation.

8 Behold! I go towards the East, but He is not there;
 And towards the West, but I discern Him not.

9 Northward I diligently seek Him, but apprehend Him not.
 The South enshroudeth Him, and I see Him not.

10 But He knoweth the path that I take;
 When He has tried me, I shall come forth as gold.

11 In His footsteps have I fixed my feet;
 His way have I kept, and have not turned aside.

12 From the command of His lips also I have not departed;
 In my bosom have I treasured up the words of His mouth.

13 But He is unchangeable, and who can turn Him?
   As His will listeth, so He accomplishes.

14 Truly the decree concerning me He will fulfil,
   And many such decrees rest with Him.

15 Therefore am I confounded at His presence;
   I ponder in my heart, and tremble because of Him.

16 Yea, God hath made my heart faint,
   And the Almighty hath confounded me.

17 Because I perished not before darkness came,
   Yea, before thick darkness had enshrouded me.

CHAPTER XXIV.

1 Why are not times of judgment reserved in store by the Almighty?
   And why do not they who know Him see His days of vengeance?

2 Men remove landmarks;
   They steal a flock and depasture it.

3 The orphan's ass they drive away,
   The widow's ox they distrain.

4 The needy they thrust aside out of the way,
   The oppressed of the land are made to hide themselves together.

5 Behold, as wild asses in the desert
   Go they forth to their pursuits,

   Rising early for the pillage of the wilderness,
   Food for each one of them and for their children.

6 In land not their own they harvest,
   And the vineyard they iniquitously crop.

7 The naked they make to pass the night without clothing,
   And without covering in the cold,

8 Who are drenched with mountain-storm,
   And cleave to the rock for want of shelter.

9 The fatherless they pluck from the breast,
   And from the poor exact a pledge;

10 They make him to go naked without a garment,
   And they that are famishing carry the sheaves of corn.
11 These express oil within their walls,
   They tread their vine-vats, and yet suffer thirst.
12 From anguish the dying groan,
   And the soul of the wounded crieth out,
   And God heedeth not prayer.
13 These are they who rebel against the light,
   They ignore the progress thereof,
   And in its course they abide not.
14 At day-dawn riseth the murderer,
   He slays the poor and needy,
   And by night he acts the thief.
15 For the twilight watcheth also the eye of the adulterer,
   Saying, "No eye shall see me,"
   And covers his face with a muffler.
16 In the dark he diggeth through houses,
   In the day-time such seal themselves up,
   They are strangers to the light.
17 For the morning they reckon to themselves as the death-shade,
   Because it maketh known to them the horrors of the death-shade.
18 Cursed is he on the face of the waters,
   Accursed is the lot of such upon the earth;
   He regardeth not the treading of the vineyards.
19 Drought and heat consume the snow-waters,
   So does Sheol those who have sinned.
20 The womb will forget him,
   The worm will feed sweetly on him.

   He will no more be remembered,
   And iniquity shall be shivered as a tree.
21 This one despoileth the barren that beareth not,
   And to the widow dealeth no good.
22 The mighty also he pulleth down by his power,
   He riseth up, and no one is secure of life.

23 (God) grants to him security, and he is sustained,
But His eyes are upon their ways.

24 They are exalted for a little time, and then are not;
They perish, like all others they die,
And are cut off like the topmost ears of corn.

25 And is not this the case? Who then can confute me?
And set my words at nought?

CHAP. XXIII. VER. 6. *Set His heart upon me.*—The words, HIS HEART, are not expressed, but understood, as in iv. 20. The meaning is: He would deliberately consider my case. He would rightly estimate my past life, and the judgment I am now suffering. He would compassionate my sufferings, and set His heart on me to deliver me.

VERS. 13, 14. These verses affirm, that the sufferings of Job, inflicted by the malignity of Satan, resulted from God's eternal immutable purpose before the foundation of the world. These verses further teach, that the administration of the universe is not contingent on fate, or chance, or the volitions and passions of fallen man, but is regulated by the sovereign will of Him without whose fiat not a sparrow can die, or a hair can fall from our heads, without whose permission Satan himself is powerless in that world of which he is God, ruling in the children of disobedience.

"Sovereign Ruler of the skies,
Ever gracious, ever wise!
All my times are in Thy hand,
All events at Thy command.

His decree, who form'd the earth,
Fix'd my first and second birth;
Parents, native place, and time,
All appointed were by Him.

He that form'd me in the womb,
He shall guide me to the tomb;
All my times shall ever be
Order'd by His wise decree.

Times of sickness, times of health,
Times of penury and wealth,
Times of trial and of grief,
Times of triumph and relief,

Times the Tempter's power to prove,
Times to taste a Saviour's love;—
All must come, and last, and end,
As shall please my Heavenly Friend."—*Dr. Ryland.*

CHAP. XXIV. VER. 13. *Course.*—The Hebrew noun is plural, but the English singular expresses the exact meaning of the Hebrew plural. This is one of the many instances wherein literality of rendering would impair the sense.

VERS. 18-25. The obscurity of the last verses of this chapter, arising partly from Job's rapid transition from one subject to another, and from constant change from singular to plural and from plural to singular, has been acknowledged by all who have critically examined the original Hebrew, and is self-evident from the endless diversity of the interpretations which have been proposed. The accurate and learned Schultens, to whom the world is so deeply indebted for his successful elucidation of the Book of Job, comments most energetically on the difficulty of understanding and translating these verses. See his candid statements of hesitation and doubt in his efforts to unravel these difficulties in the Critical Appendix.

THIRD SPEECH OF BILDAD THE SHUHITE.

CHAPTER XXV.

Bildad, in reply to Job's expressed desire, that God would adjudicate his case and vindicate his integrity, briefly asserts the omnipotence, omniscience, omnipresence, and sovereignty of Jehovah, and argues therefrom that sinful man cannot justify himself in the sight of a heart-searching God, and that the Judge of all the earth must do right at all times, on all occasions, and towards all men.

1 Then responded Bildad the Shuhite, and said:

2 Dominion and fear are with Him;
  He in his heavenly places executeth retributive justice.

3 Are not His hosts innumerable?
  And upon whom doth not His light shine?

4 How then can mortal man be justified before God?
  And how can he of woman born be pure?

5 Look to the moon, which He hath not made stationary,
  And to the stars, these are not pure in His eyes.

6 How much less mortal man—a worm,
  And the son of man—a reptile?

CHAP. XXV. VER. 5. *The moon He hath not made stationary.*—Literally, HE HATH NOT PITCHED ITS TENT. From the circumstance of many Orientals habitually dwelling in tents, the Hebrew word rendered TENT in many texts designates a stationary abode or fixed dwelling-place (see Joshua xxii. 4, 6-8; 2 Samuel xviii. 17, xix. 8; 1 Kings xii. 16; Malachi ii. 12). Hence the poetic imagery employed by Bildad clearly indicates that the moon, or lunar light, was not stationary. Though the Bible is not designed to impart scientific knowledge, yet there is more of true science in the Bible than is generally imagined. The scientific statements of Scripture proceed from the inspiration of the God of nature, and in themselves, and for their designed use, are infallibly correct, however they may be misinterpreted, misunderstood, maligned, and contemptuously rejected. The Hebrew word rendered MOON, signifies the lunar light, or the light reflected from the orb of the moon, rather than the orb of the moon itself. "God hath caused no tent to be pitched for it. It is always increasing and diminishing, having no settled place to renew its light; but the solar light hath, which therefore shines always regularly." Bates' *Hebrew Lexicon*. "God hath not fixed the tent of the moon. The lunar light has no fixed tabernacle, but the orb which reflects it revolves round the sun in company with the earth, and, from this complex motion, is to the inhabitants of the earth sometimes luminous, sometimes partly dark, and sometimes totally so. If then the lunar light, that beauteous and even idolized object, thus changeth and decreaseth in, or upon, her perfection, or rather till it disappears, and the stars be not pure in His sight, how much less shall man be perfect and sinless?"—Parkhurst's *Hebrew Lexicon*.

REPLY OF JOB TO THE THIRD SPEECH OF BILDAD.

CHAPTER XXVI.

Job rebuketh Bildad, because he had not been active for God in his day and generation.

Job professeth his own faith in the Divine perfections manifested by God in the intermediate state of departed spirits; in the creation, preservation, and administration of the universe; in the rainbow, the symbol of God's everlasting covenant with Noah and his posterity; in the luminaries which bespangle the sky; and in Messiah's final bruising of the head of that old serpent the Devil, who had tempted Adam and Eve in Paradise, had despoiled Job of his family and property, had afflicted him with the loathsome elephantiasis, and who now goeth about seeking whom he may devour.

1 Then responded Job, and said:

2 How hast thou helped the powerless?
   How hast thou succoured the arm devoid of strength?

3 How hast thou counselled the unwise?
   And how hast thou imparted wisdom to the multitude?

4 Whose sayings hast thou repeated?
   And whose inspiration hath proceeded from thee?

5 Apostate spirits are tormented,
   Beneath the waters and their inhabitants.

6 Sheol is naked before Him,
   And Perdition hath no covering.

7 He stretcheth out the northern hemisphere over empty space,
   He suspends the globe upon nothing.

8 He binds up the waters in His dark clouds,
   And the cloud is not rent under them.

9 He shutteth up the appearance of His throne,
   He spreadeth His dense clouds over it.

10 He hath ordained a bow over the face of the waters,
    To the confines of light and darkness.

11 The columns of heaven vibrate,
    And are astounded at his restraint.

12 By his might He stilleth the sea,
  And by His wisdom He scourgeth its pride.
13 By His spirit He hath garnished the heavens,
  His hand hath wounded the fugitive serpent.
14 Lo! these are the outlines of His ways;
  And how small is the portion of matter understood therein?
  But the thunder of His power, O who can understand?

CHAP. XXVI. VER. 5. *Apostate spirits.*—Death is the separation of soul and body. After death the body returns to its original element of dust. It is too generally imagined, that the soul of the believer ascends IMMEDIATELY after death to heaven, and that the soul of the Christless sinner descends IMMEDIATELY after death to hell. But the doctrine of the Bible is that disembodied spirits exist between death and their resurrection in an intermediate state, called SHEOL in the Hebrew of the Old Testament, and HADES in the Greek of the New Testament, in which state the saved repose in felicity on Abraham's bosom, and the lost are incipiently tormented. The Hebrew word, mistranslated in our Authorized Version DEAD THINGS, has a threefold signification in Hebrew. It signifies, firstly, a Canaanitish tribe, the Rephaim, beyond Jordan, celebrated for their gigantic stature: Genesis xiv. 5, xv. 20; Deuteronomy ii. 11-20, iii. 13; Joshua xv. 8, xviii. 16; 2 Samuel v. 18, 22, xxiii. 13; 1 Chronicles xi. 15, xiv. 9; Isaiah xvii. 5. It signifies, secondly, the disembodied spirits of the dead generally: Psalm lxxxviii. 11 (10); Isaiah xiv. 9, xxvi. 14, 19. It signifies, thirdly, the disembodied spirits of the apostate dead: Proverbs ii. 18, ix. 18, xxi. 16. Joseph Mede thus comments on this signification:—"The place where the old GIANTS mourn or wail under the waters, and their fellow-inhabitants, the rest of the damned with them, even INFERNUS, and the place of perdition itself, is naked and open to the eyes of God, from whom nothing is hid." The third signification is the meaning in this verse, which defines the locality of Sheol or Hades as beneath the crust of the earth, beneath the lowest ocean depths. This is substantiated by the ascent of the disembodied spirit of Samuel to Saul from Sheol to the cave of Endor. As this earth is the theatre of man's probation, so is it the theatre of the intermediate state of disembodied spirits, between their death and their resurrection, and so will it be the theatre of the glorification of saints, who shall be kings and priests UPON EARTH for one thousand years, when Christ shall reign King of Kings and Lord of Lords.

VER. 7. "In that excellent Book of Job, if it be revolved with diligence, it will be found pregnant and swelling with natural philosophy; as, for example, cosmography and the roundness of the world; wherein the pensileness of the earth, the pole of the north, and the finiteness or convexity of heaven are manifestly touched."—*Lord Bacon, quoted by Bishop Wordsworth.*

VER. 11. *The columns of heaven.*—See Note on ix. 6.

VER. 13. *The fugitive serpent.*—The context evidently implies, that this verse has reference to some being who once was or is now in heaven, and not to any animal real or imaginary, terrestrial or aquatic. Two reasons may be assigned why the serpent of this verse cannot designate the sign of the zodiac so called. 1. There is no reason to believe that the signs of the zodiac were known in the age when Job lived, at least by the names they now bear. 2. No cause can be assigned why the serpent of the zodiac should be designated FLYING or FUGITIVE. The LXX. and Coptic versions render THE APOSTATE SERPENT, namely, that old serpent the Devil, who tempted Adam and Eve in Paradise, and the incarnate Son of God in the wilderness, and whose malignity inflicted upon Job all his sufferings. Well may he be called FUGITIVE, from his expulsion out of heaven. "And the great dragon was cast out, that old serpent called the Devil and Satan, which deceiveth the whole world: he was cast out into the earth, and his angels are cast out with him."—*Revelation* xii. 9. The wounding of Satan is predicted, Genesis iii. 15 and Romans xvi. 20. It is true that the composition of Genesis is posterior in time to the composition of the Book of Job, but the same predictive curse which was revealed to the author of Genesis, may also have been antecedently revealed to the author of Job, whoever that author may have been. "If we render the Hebrew verb *perfodit, vulnerarit* (WOUNDED), the place will allude to Genesis iii. 14, 15, and it is paraphrased in Isaiah xxvii. 1, where we have a manifest prediction of the coming and victories of Christ, and where this very fugitive serpent is said to be pierced with a sword."—*Lee.*

JOB'S PAUSE, AND SUBSEQUENT RESUMPTION OF HIS ARGUMENT.

CHAPTERS XXVII. AND XXVIII.

At the conclusion of chapter xxvi. Job paused, awaiting the third speech which he expected from Zophar, the Naamathite, whose turn it was to have spoken. Zophar remaining silent, Job continued his self-vindication.

Job piously resolves, notwithstanding all his agonizing sufferings, to remain constant and immoveable in faith and integrity. He recounts and repels the traditionary sayings inaptly quoted against him. He records man's successful prosecution of mining and metallurgy, and consequent possession of silver, gold, and precious stones, but extols the wisdom which is from above as beyond all price, and as exclusively God's gift to sinful man.

BEHOLD, THE FEAR OF JEHOVAH, THAT IS WISDOM ;
AND TO DEPART FROM EVIL IS UNDERSTANDING.

1 Then Job resumed his discourse, and said :

2 As God liveth, who hath set aside my right of judgment,
 Even the Almighty who hath embittered my soul,

3 So long as my breath is in me,
 And the spirit of God is in my nostrils,

4 Never shall my lips speak wickedness,
 Nor my tongue utter deceit.

5 Far be it from me, that I should justify you ;
 I will not cast away mine integrity from me even unto death.

6 To my righteousness I adhere, and will not relinquish it ;
 My heart shall not be reproached for my (past) days.

7 My enemy shall be accounted as unrighteous,
 And he that riseth up against me as wicked.

8 For what is the hope of the profane when God shall cut off,
 When God shall unsheath, his soul ?

9 Will God listen to his cry,
 When distress shall come upon him ?

10 He doth not delight himself in the Almighty ;
 He doth not call upon God continually.

11 I will instruct you concerning the operation of God,
   That which is with the Almighty I will not withhold.

12 Behold, yourselves, all of you, have witnessed it;
   Why then do ye babble these babblings?

13 " This is the portion of a wicked man from God,
   And the heritage of oppressors which they receive from the Almighty.

14 If his children multiply, the sword shall be upon them,
   And his offspring shall not be satisfied with bread.

15 His survivors shall be sepulchred by death,
   And his widows shall make no lamentation.

16 Should he hoard silver as the dust,
   And lay up raiment as the mire?

17 He may lay it up, but the just shall wear it,
   And the innocent shall divide the silver.

18 He buildeth his house like the moth-worm,
   Or as a booth which the vineyard-keeper constructeth.

19 The rich man lieth down, and taketh nothing (with him);
   He openeth his eyes, and he is not.

20 Terrors shall overtake him like waters;
   In the night a tempest shall sweep him away.

21 The east wind carries him off, and he is gone,
   And tempestuously storms him from his place.

22 Yea, it driveth upon him, and spareth not,
   That he should escape from its power by flight.

23 It claps its (tempest) hands at him,
   And hisses him away out of his place."

CHAPTER XXVIII.

1 Verily there is a mine from whence they extract the silver ore,
   And a place where they refine gold.

2 Iron is taken out of the earth,
   And stone-ore is smelted into copper.

3 Man putteth an end to darkness,
  And searcheth out to the utmost limit
  The stones of darkness and the death-shade.

4 He sinks a shaft far from human habitation,
  Oblivious of the foot they hang suspended,
  Afar from mortal man, they swing to and fro.

5 From out of the earth is produced corn,
  And its lower strata turned up resemble fire.

6 Its stones are the place of sapphires,
  And gold-dust is therein.

7 The pathway thereto no bird of prey hath espied,
  Nor has the vulture's eye glanced on it.

8 The (forest) sons of pride have not trodden it,
  Nor the black-maned lion passed over it.

9 Against the flinty rock man extendeth his hand,
  He overturneth mountains from their base.

10 Through the rocks he cutteth out channels of water,
   And his eye inspecteth every precious thing.

11 He restraineth the waters from oozing,
   And hidden treasures he bringeth forth to light.

12 But from whence shall wisdom be found?
   And where is the abode of understanding?

13 Man knoweth not its worth,
   Nor is it found in the land of the living.

14 The deep saith, "It is not in me,"
   And the sea saith, "It is not with me."

15 Refined gold cannot be given in exchange for it,
   Nor can silver be weighed out for its purchase.

16 It cannot be estimated by the ingot of Ophir,
   By the precious onyx or the sapphire.

17 Neither gold nor the diamond can compete with it,
   Nor for vessels of pure gold can it be bartered.

18 Rock-crystal and pearls cannot be mentioned,
    Yea, to draw forth wisdom is more than rubies can do.

19 The topaz of Cush cannot be compared with it,
    Nor with the pure ingot can it be bartered.

20 From whence then cometh wisdom?
    Yea, where is the dwelling-place of understanding?

21 Since it is hidden from the eyes of all living,
    And concealed from the birds of heaven.

22 Perdition and Death say:
    "We have heard of the fame thereof with our ears."

23 God (alone) giveth understanding of the way to it,
    For He knoweth its dwelling-place.

24 For He seeth to the extremities of the earth,
    And surveyeth (all) under the whole heaven.

25 When to the wind he had prescribed weight,
    And had regulated the waters by measure;

26 When He had made a decree for the rain,
    And a pathway for the thunder-flash;

27 Then He saw it, and declared it;
    He established it, and investigated it.

28 And unto Adam He said:
    "𝔅𝔢𝔥𝔬𝔩𝔡, 𝔱𝔥𝔢 𝔣𝔢𝔞𝔯 𝔬𝔣 𝔍𝔢𝔥𝔬𝔳𝔞𝔥, 𝔱𝔥𝔞𝔱 𝔦𝔰 𝔴𝔦𝔰𝔡𝔬𝔪;
    𝔄𝔫𝔡 𝔱𝔬 𝔡𝔢𝔭𝔞𝔯𝔱 𝔣𝔯𝔬𝔪 𝔢𝔳𝔦𝔩 𝔦𝔰 𝔲𝔫𝔡𝔢𝔯𝔰𝔱𝔞𝔫𝔡𝔦𝔫𝔤."

CHAP. XXVII. VER. 14. *His children.*—"The Targum paraphrases it HIS CHILDREN'S CHILDREN, and so Sephorno, to which agrees the Latin Version."—*Dr. Gill.*

VER. 15. *His widows.*—Not the mere widow of the wicked man, but the widows pertaining to the family, especially the widows of the survivors sepulchred by death.

VER. 19. *He opens his eyes.*—"In hell (Hades) the rich man lifted up his eyes, being in torments."—(*Luke* xvi. 23).

VER. 23. *The east wind claps its tempest hands at him, and hisses him away out of his place.*—This is perhaps the boldest and most beautiful prosopopœia even in oriental poetry. Schultens thus comments upon its beauties: -"Venusta, non minus quam gravis, figura. VENTUS PLAUDIT ALAS, COMPLODIT MANUS, QUANDO VEHEMENTI SONO FERTUR, ET OMNIA PER AURAS VERRIT. IDEM EXSIBILAT VELUTI QUÆ RAPIDO ET STRIDENTE TURBINE AUFERT E SUIS SEDIBUS."

CHAP. XXVIII. VERS. 1, 6, 15-17. *Gold.*—Four different Hebrew terms are employed in these verses to signify GOLD, apparently designating it according to its degrees of purity. This gold was evidently the product of Arabia. The navy of Solomon and Hiram "brought gold (into Palestine) from Ophir" (in Arabia) (1 *Kings* x. 11). Solomon also received gold from "all the kings of Arabia" (1 *Kings* x. 15). "Silver was nothing accounted of in the days of Solomon." Solomon's importation of gold from Ophir and Tarshish "in one year was six hundred threescore and six talents" (1 *Kings* x. 14). At present no mines of gold or silver are worked in Arabia. Arabia, once so prolific of gold, now exhibits neither gold mines nor auriferous sands. Niebuhr testifies :—" Il se peut que les Grecs ayant anciennement trouvé beaucoup d'or en Arabie—on ne trouve aucun or en Arabie, ni dans les rivières, ni dans les mines." Did the ancients exhaust the gold mines and auriferous sands of Arabia ? or do the present inhabitants of Arabia want skill and appliances to extract from their soil the precious metal ?

VER. 2. *Copper.*—" Copper, native brass. It may not be improper to remark here, that what we commonly call BRASS, and the French CUIVRE JAUNE, yellow copper, is a factitious metal composed of copper and *lapis calaminaris*"—Parkhurst's *Hebrew Lexicon*. "The allusion to the process by which it was obtained clearly implies, that the smelting of copper from the ore was known at the period when the Book of Job was composed. It should be understood, then, that when reference is made to the ore, or to the metal in its original state, not BRASS, but COPPER is the word that should be employed."—Fairbairn's *Bible Dictionary*.

VER. 5. *Its lower strata turned up resemble fire.*—The lower strata of the earth are akin to the colour of fire, from the sapphires and other precious stones, and from the gold and other metals, found therein.

VER. 7. *The vulture's eye.*—The Hebrew noun here rendered VULTURE seems employed in this passage as a generic term to comprehend all raptorial birds, especially the various species of the eagle, the vulture, and the kite.

VER. 8. *Sons of pride*—This oriental phrase occurs only in this verse and in xli. 26 (34) ; and signifies the largest, the fiercest, the most savage animals, terrestrial and aquatic. The word (forest) is here added to make the sense clear and intelligible.

VER. 17. *Diamonds.*—It is singular that in the Authorized Version, and in almost all versions, of this chapter, the diamond should not be named in this enumeration of the most precious stones known to the ancients. The Hebrew word, from its etymology, evidently signifies a transparent and hyaline gem. I follow Luther in interpreting it DIAMONDS.

JOB'S SECOND PAUSE, AND SUBSEQUENT RESUMPTION OF HIS ARGUMENT.

CHAPTERS XXIX., XXX., AND XXXI.

At the conclusion of chapter xxviii. Job paused a second time, waiting to see whether any one of his three friends would continue their argumentation. All three remained silent. Job then continued his self-vindication.

Job contrasts his past prosperity with his present degradation and misery, prays to God to answer his supplications and vindicate his cause, and makes this solemn appeal to the Searcher of hearts:

WHAT IS MY PORTION ? GOD MOST HIGH.
WHAT IS MINE INHERITANCE ? THE ALMIGHTY SUPREME.

1 Then again Job resumed his discourse, and said :

2 O that I were as in former months !
 As in days when God protected me !

3 When He caused His lamp to shine over my head,
 By His light I walked through darkness.

4 As I was in my autumn days,
 When the counsel of God was over my tabernacle.

5 While yet the Almighty was with me,
   My children were round about me.

6 When my footsteps were bathed in cream,
   And the rock poured out by me rivers of oil.

7 When I went forth to the gate of the city,
   And placed my seat at the forum.

8 The young men saw me and retired,
   And the elders rose up and stood.

9 The rulers refrained from speaking,
   And laid their hands on their mouths.

10 The chiefs suppressed their voice,
   And their tongue cleaved to the roof of their mouth.

11 When the ear heard me, then it blessed me;
   And when the eye saw me, then it witnessed for me.

12 Because I delivered the poor that cried,
   The orphan, and him that had no helper.

13 The blessing of him that was ready to perish came upon me,
   And I caused the widow's heart to sing for joy.

14 I put on righteousness, and it clothed me,
   My rectitude was to me for mantle and turban.

15 I was eyes to the blind,
   And feet was I to the lame.

16 I was a father to the indigent,
   And the cause which I understood not I searched out.

17 And I broke the grinders of the wicked,
   And plucked the spoil from his teeth.

18 Then said I: "I shall die in my nest,
   And shall multiply days as the sand.

19 My roots are outspread by the waters,
   And the dew lodges all night on my branches.

20 My glory is unfading around me,
   And my bow shall be renewed in my hand."

21 To me men gave ear and waited,
   Yea, they silently awaited my counsel.
22 After my words they replied not,
   And my speech distilled upon them as dew.
23 Yea, they waited for me as for the rain,
   And opened their mouths wide, as for the latter rain.
24 Smiled I upon them? they were incredulous,
   And the light of my countenance they could not cast down.
25 I directed their course, and presided as chief,
   And dwelt as monarch over the host,
   As comforter of the grief-oppressed.

CHAPTER XXX.

1 But now they deride me,
   Who in years are younger than myself.

  Whose fathers I disdained
  To rank with the dogs of my flock.

2 Yea, the strength of their hands how can it profit me,
  They, in whom completion of vigour hath perished,
3 Through destitution and famine of the rock?

  Who were yesterday gnawers of the desert,
  Of the waste, and the wilderness,

4 Plucking the sea-purslain from the underwood,
  And the root of the genista-broom for their food.

5 From society they are driven
  (Men shout after them as after a thief)

6 To dwell in horrid glens,
  In caves of the earth and in rocks.

7 They bray among the bushes,
  Beneath the prickly acanthus they are gathered together.

8 Children of crime, yea, children of infamy,
  They were scourged from the land.

9 But now I have become their song,
　Yea, I have become a bye-word among them.
10 They abominate me, they stand aloof from me,
　They forbear not to spit before my face.
11 For each one lets loose all restraint, and afflicts me,
　And they cast away the curb (of deference) in my presence.
12 On the right hand riseth up a youngster brood,
　My feet they thrust aside,
　They cast up against me ways whereby they may destroy me.
13 They break up my pathway,
　They help forward my ruin,
　There is no help against them.
14 Like a vast breaker they rush on,
　Tempest-like they roll themselves tumultuously onwards,
15 Utter destruction is turned upon me.
　My dignity is chased away like the wind,
　And my security has passed away like a cloud.
16 And now my soul is dissolved within me.
　Days of affliction have taken hold of me.
17 By night my bones within me are corroded,
　And my gnawing pains cease not.
18 With great force must my garment be stripped off,
　It entwines me like the collar of my vest.
19 He hath cast me into the mire,
　And I am become like dust and ashes.
20 I cry unto Thee, but Thou answerest not,
　I persevere, but Thou regardest me not,
21 Thou art changed into an implacable enemy unto me,
　With thy powerful hand Thou dost persecute me,
22 Thou upliftest me into the whirlwind, and waftest me away,
　And Thou utterly dissolvest my substance.
23 Behold! I know that Thou wilt bring me to death,
　And to the house appointed for all living.

24 Howbeit not to my grave will He extend His hand,
Surely by its destruction He vouchsafes salvation.

25 Should I not weep, as one whose life is grievous?
Should not my soul be sorrowful, as one afflicted?

26 When I looked for good, then came evil;
When I waited for light, then came darkness.

27 My bowels boil and have no rest;
Days of affliction have overtaken me.

28 I go blackened, but not with sun-heat;
I stand in the congregation: I pour out my lamentations.

29 I am become a brother to jackalls,
And a companion to the ostrich-brood.

30 My skin is black upon me,
And my bones burn with heat.

31 My harp is turned to lamentation,
And my pipe to the voice of them that weep.

CHAPTER XXXI.

1 I have made a covenant with mine eyes,
In what manner then should I look upon a maid?

2 And what is (my) portion? God most high.
And what is (mine) inheritance? The Almighty supreme.

3 Is not destruction (ordained) for the wicked?
And alienation (from God) for workers of iniquity?

4 He, does He not see my ways?
And number all my footsteps?

5 If I have walked with unfaithfulness,
And if my foot hath hastened towards deceit,

6 Let Him weigh me in the scales of justice,
And let God discriminate mine integrity.

7 If my footsteps have turned aside from the way,
And if my heart have gone after my eyes,
And if a stain have cleaved to the palms of my hands,

8 Then may I sow, and another eat,
    And may the produce of my lands be rooted up.

9 If my heart have been enticed towards a woman,
    Or if I have laid wait at my neighbour's door,

10 Then let my wife grind for another,
    And let others crouch down upon her.

11 For this is a grievous crime,
    Yea, it is iniquity for judicial infliction.

12 For this is a fire consuming to destruction,
    And which would root out all my increase.

13 If I have spurned the right of my man-servant or of my maid
    In their litigations with me,

14 Then what shall I do when God shall arise,
    And when He shall judge, what shall I answer unto Him?

15 Did not He who made me in the womb make him?
    And did not the same one fashion us in the matrix?

16 If I have withheld the poor from employment,
    Or have caused the eyes of the widow to fail;

17 Or if I have eaten my morsel myself alone,
    And the orphan hath not eaten thereof

18 (For from my youth grief hath disciplined me,
    And from my mother's womb I have been compassionate);

19 If I have seen one perishing for want of clothing,
    Or that to the needy there was no covering,

20 If his loins have not blessed me,
    And if he has not been warmed from the fleece of my lambs;

21 If I have shaken my hand against the orphan,
    When I saw my help in the gate,—

22 May my shoulder fall from its shoulder-blade,
    And mine arm be dissevered from its socket.

23 For destruction from God was a terror to me,
    And before His majesty I was powerless to do it.

24 If I have made gold my dependence,
   Or said to the ingot, "Thou art my confidence;"

25 If I have exulted because my wealth was increased,
   Or because my hand had gotten abundance;

38 If my own land cry out against me,
   And its furrows weep together;

39 If I have eaten its produce without wages,
   Or caused its managers to lose their life;

40 Let the star-thistle grow up instead of wheat,
   And the aconite instead of barley.

26 If I looked on the sun when it shone,
   Or the moon progressing in radiance,

27 And my heart hath secretly been beguiled,
   And my mouth hath kissed my hand;

28 This also were an iniquity for judicial punishment,
   For I should have denied God most high.

29 If I have rejoiced in the destruction of him that hated me,
   And exulted when evil befel him

30 (Yea, I have not suffered my mouth to sin,
   To imprecate a curse on his soul):

31 If the men of my tent have not said:
   "Is there one who hath not been full fed with his meat?"

32 (The stranger never passed the night in the street,
   My doors I opened to the traveller.)

33 If like Adam I have suppressed my transgressions,
   By hiding mine iniquity in my bosom,

34 Then let me be confounded before the grand assembly,
   And let the contempt of the clans crush me,
   Yea, let me be struck dumb, let me never go forth at the door.

35 Oh that He would grant me a hearing!
   Behold my gage! Oh that the Almighty would answer me,
   And that mine adversary would write down (his) charge!

36 Surely, I would carry it on my shoulder,
   And bind it upon me as a diadem!
37 The whole of my footsteps would I disclose to Him,
   And would reverentially approach Him as Supreme.

CHAP. XXIX. VERS. 11-17.—To illustrate Job's conduct to his fellow-men, detailed in these verses in self-exculpation, I append the Table of Moral Maxims extracted by Bridel from the Book of Job—maxims which none can read without edification and profit.

DE DIEU.

Il y a un seul Dieu, qui a créé les cieux et la terre; tu le serviras.
Tu ne porteras point ta main à ta bouche en l'honneur du soleil et de la lune.
La crainte de Dieu est la véritable science.

DU RESPECT POUR LES VIEILLARDS.

La sagesse est dans les viellards.
L'expérience est le fruit des longues années.
Que le jeune homme se taise devant les cheveux blancs.
Que les enfants se cachent à l'approchement des anciens.

DU MEURTRE.

Tu ne tueras point.
Tu ne blesseras personne à mort.
Tu ne te tueras pas toi-même.

DE L'ADULTÈRE.

Tu ne commettras point d'adultère.
Tu ne commettras pas le péché contre nature.
Tu feras une alliance avec les yeux, pour ne pas les arrêter sur une vierge.

DU VOL.

Tu ne deroberas point.
Tu ne voleras ni sur les grands chemins ni dans le désert.
Tu ne perceras point les maisons de nuit.
Tu ne raviras pas l'enfant qui est à la mamelle.
Tu n'enlevras pas le bétail qui est sur les pâturages.
Tu ne remueras pas les bornes.
Ote l'interdit qui est dans ta maison.

DU MENSONGE.

Tu ne mentiras point.
Tu n'useras point de fraude ou de tromperie.
Tu n'ouvriras pas une fosse devant ton ami.

DU GAGE.

Tu ne prendras point de gage du pauvre.
Tu ne prendras point en gage le bœuf de la veuve.
Tu n'emmeneras pas l'âne de l'orphelin.
Tu ne chasseras pas dans le désert le débiteur insolvable.

DEVOIR DU JUGE.

Tu ne recevras point de présent pour pervertir le droit.
Tu ne fausseras pas la règle de la justice.
Tu ne regarderas pas à l'apparence des personnes.

DE L'ÉQUITÉ.

Tu feras droit à ton serviteur et ta servante.
Tu ne retiendras point le salaire de l'ouvrier.
Tu ne mangeras pas du produit du champ avant de l'avoir payé.
Celui qui porte tes gerbes n'aura pas faim.
Celui qui presse ton huile n'aura pas soif.

De l'Aumône.

Tu feras l'aumône.
Tu ne chasseras pas le pauvre du chemin.
Tu donneras du pain à celui qui a faim.
Tu donneras de l'eau à celui qui est fatigué du voyage.
Tu habilleras le nécessiteux de la laine de tes moutons.
Tu élèveras l'orphelin auprès de toi.
Tu ne renverras pas une veuve à vide.

De l'Hospitalité.

Tu ne fermeras pas ta porte à l'étranger et au voyageur.
Tu ne souffriras pas qu'ils passent la nuit dans la rue.
Tu ne mangeras pas seul les morceaux de ta table.

Devoir du Goël.

Tu es le Goël de tes proches.
Tu vengeras leur sang répandu sans cause.
Tu vengeras toute injure qui leur sera faite.
Tu les rachèteras de la main de leur ennemi.

De la Protection du Faible.

Tu n'opprimeras pas le faible en jugement sous la porte.
Tu défendras la cause de l'étranger et de l'orphelin.
Tu poursuivras le ravisseur, et tu lui enlèveras sa proie d'entre les dents.

Résistance à l'Oppression.

Tu ne souffriras pas que les violents s'emparent du pays.

Du Pardon des Injures.

Tu ne maudiras point ton ennemi.
Tu ne desireras pas qu'il meure.
Tu ne te réjouiras pas de son malheur.

De la Colère.

Garde-toi de la colère; elle tue l'insensé.

De la Convoitise.

Garde-toi de la convoitise des yeux,
Et de l'orgueil des richesses,
Et d'une folle joie quand tes biens sont multipliés.

Offices de l'Humanité.

Tu consoleras les affligés.
Tu visiteras les malades.
Tu n'abandonneras pas le lépreux.
Tu seras les yeux de l'aveugle et les pieds du boiteux.
Tu ne jetteras pas le filet sur celui qui n'a plus de père.

These maxims were acknowledged and practised by many who lived more than 2000 years before the advent of the predicted Messiah. Their religious knowledge could alone have been derived from the uncertainty of tradition and the still small voice of the Spirit, vouchsafed to the prayer of faith. On these ancients the bright beams of revelation had never shone. Yet their faith and conduct most favourably contrast with the faith and conduct of multitudes who are privileged to live under the midday blaze of Gospel light.

Chap. XXX. Ver. 1. *The dogs of my flock.*—From this expression it is self-evident, that sheep-dogs of some canine species were extensively employed in the days of Job in North-Western Arabia, for the same purpose as sheep-dogs are now kept in England and elsewhere.

Ver. 24. *Salvation.*—Job anticipated that glory, which is the result of salvation, not at the deposit of his body in the grave, but at the resurrection of his body from the grave. At the resurrection of his body and its reunion with his previously disembodied spirit, he expected salvation from separation of soul and body—salvation from annihilation of body, resulting from its return to its original dust—salvation from sin, death, and hell—salvation from all the effects and consequences of man's fall in Adam. "When this corruptible shall have put on incorruption, and this mortal shall have put on immortality, then shall be brought to pass the saying that is written: Death is swallowed up in victory" (1 *Corinthians* xv. 54). "I will ransom them from the power of Sheol, I will redeem them from death" (*Hosea* xiii. 14).

CHAP. XXXI. VER. 1. *I have made a covenant with mine eyes.*—"Job was not an Israelite, but a Gentile, and yet he knew that fornication was a sin, and shunned and detested it, as contrary to God's primeval legislation; and his words here are a protest against the licentiousness of heathen nations in this particular, and still more against the lax notions and practices of some who live under the Gospel."—*Bishop Wordsworth.*

VER. 18.—The meaning I deduce from this verse is this, that sanctified affliction from his earliest years had been blessed to Job, and that from his own sufferings, corporeal or mental, it had caused him to feel sympathy and compassion for the poor, the stranger, the fatherless, and the widow. Sanctified affliction is frequently used by God as an instrument to bring sinners out of nature's darkness to the saving light and power of Divine truth, but is also graciously employed to humble God's children in the dust, to bring their past sins to remembrance, to strengthen their faith, to purify their motives, to augment their self-devotion and usefulness, and to make them more meet for the inheritance of the saints in glory. For the explanation of the critical difficulty of this obscure passage the reader is referred to the Critical Appendix.

VERS. 38-40.—"This defence now concludes with six lines; which declare—that, if he had either enjoyed his estates COVETOUSLY, or procured them UNJUSTLY, he wished them to prove BARREN and UNPROFITABLE. This part therefore seems naturally to follow verse 25, where he speaks of his gold, and how much his hand had gotten."—Kennicott's *Posthumous Remarks.* "I cannot but be of opinion with Heath and Scott, that the passage stands in its wrong place at the end of the chapter."—*Fry.* "A small degree of attention will, I imagine, convince any one that the speech ended with the foregoing verse (37). These verses therefore are out of their original situation. They would enter properly among the articles of injustice." —*Scott.*

SPEECH OF ELIHU.

CHAPTERS XXXII., XXXIII., XXXIV., XXXV., XXXVI., AND XXXVII.

ELIHU *condemns the speeches both of Job and of his friends, and refutes their arguments.*

He teaches that inspiration from above, and not length of years or human learning, can alone communicate the wisdom which is from above,—that wisdom which saves the soul, and delivers from the wrath to come.

He affirms his own possession of perfection of knowledge (xxxvi. 4), *to which perfection of knowledge none of the fallen posterity of Adam, not even the holiest believer, can attain in his time-state here below. Job himself disowns it* (ix. 21), *saying, "I know not perfection; if I did, I myself should disown my own being."*

He asserts the sovereignty of Jehovah manifest in the sidereal heavens and in celestial phenomena, and inculcates on Job implicit submission to the Divine will.

Concluded were the words of Job,
1 And these three men ceased
From making answer to Job,
Because he was righteous in his own eyes.
2 But kindled was the wrath of ELIHU,
{ The son of Barachel, }
{ The Buzite, of the kindred of Ram, }

or { THE BLESSED SON OF GOD,
THE DESPISED ONE, OF THE LINEAGE OF THE MOST HIGH, }

2 Kindled was His anger against Job,
   Because he had justified himself before God.
3 Against his three friends His anger was also kindled,
   Because they had found no answer,
   And yet had condemned Job.
4 Now ELIHU had waited for answers to Job,
   Because in time they were older than Himself.
5 But ELIHU saw that there was no answer
   In the mouth of these three men,
   And kindled was His anger.
6 { Then answered Elihu, the son of Barachel,
   The Buzite, and said : }

or { Then answered ELIHU, THE BLESSED SON OF GOD,
THE DESPISED ONE, and said : }

   I am young in time,
   And ye are very aged,

   Therefore I shrunk back,
   And was deterred from showing you My knowledge.

7 I said : " Days should speak,
   And multitude of years should make known wisdom,

8 But the Spirit itself dwelleth in man,
   And the inspiration of the Almighty giveth them understanding.

9 It is not the great that are wise,
   Nor the aged that understand judgment;"

10 Therefore I say : " Hearken unto Me,
    I, even I Myself, will declare My knowledge.

11 Behold! I have awaited your arguments,
    I have listened to your reasonings,
    Whilst ye have been searching out words.

12 I have indeed pondered your testimonies,
    And, behold, no one hath refuted Job,
    Not one of you has answered his speeches."

13 Lest ye should say, "We have found out wisdom;"
   God, not man, hath cast him down.
14 As he has not directed his words against Me,
   So will I not reply to him with your speeches.
15 They were confounded, they responded no more,
   Words failed them.
16 So I waited, because they spake not,
   Because they were at a stand-still, and answered no more.
17 I, even I Myself, will answer on My own behalf;
   I, even I Myself, will declare My knowledge.
18 Lo! I am overcharged with words,
   The Spirit in My heart constraineth Me.
19 Behold, My heart is as wine that hath no vent,
   As new skin-bottles that are ready to burst.
20 I will speak, that I may be relieved;
   I will open My lips, and I will reply.
21 Truly I will not respect the person of man,
   Yea, I will not keep silence, I will not flatter.
22 Verily, I know not to flatter.
   Speedily will My Maker take Me away,

CHAPTER XXXIII.

1 Therefore, I pray thee, O Job, listen now to My sayings.
  And give ear to all My words.
2 Lo! now I have opened My mouth,
  My tongue has expatiated in My palate.
3 My words are the rectitude of My heart,
  And My lips speak knowledge in its purity.
4 The Spirit of God hath made Me,
  And the inspiration of the Almighty animates Me.
5 If thou art able, refute Me,
  Array thyself against Me, stand firm.
6 Behold! I am, according to thine own word, in the place of God,
  I, even I Myself, have been taken from the clay.

7 Behold! the dread of Me shall not affright thee,
   Neither shall My hand be heavy upon thee.

8 Surely thou hast spoken in Mine ears,
   And I have heard the sounds of thy words (saying):

9 "I am pure without apostasy,
   I am clean, and perverseness is not in Me.

10 Behold, He findeth occasions against Me,
   He regardeth Me as His enemy.

11 He putteth My feet in fetters,
   He watches all My ways."

12 Lo! in this thou art not justified. I will answer thee,
   That God is greater than man.

13 Wherefore contendest thou with Him?
   For He giveth not account of any of His acts.

14 For God speaketh once,
   Yea twice (man heedeth it not),

15 In a dream, in a vision of the night,
   When deep sleep falleth upon men,
   In slumberings on the bed.

16 Then He openeth the ears of men,
   And sealeth their instruction.

17 That He may turn aside man from his action,
   And withhold pride from man.

18 He preserveth him from the pestilence,
   Yea, his life from passing away by a missile.

19 Moreover, he is chastened by pain upon his bed,
   And by violent racking of his bones.

20 So that his life nauseates bread,
   And his soul dainty food.

21 His flesh wasteth away from sight,
   And his bones which were not seen become prominent.

22 Therefore he draweth nigh unto corruption,
   And his life to the dead.

L

23 Surely there is over him an angel,
   A mediator, One above a thousand,
   To make known unto man His righteousness.

24 Then shall He be gracious unto him, and shall say,
   "Deliver him from going down to corruption,
   I have found a ransom."

25 His flesh shall become fresher than a child's.
   He shall return to the days of his youth.

26 He shall pray unto God, and He will accept him,
   And cause him to behold His face with joy,
   And will render to man His righteousness.

27 He will sing before men, and will say,
   "I have sinned, and have perverted right.
   But He hath not requited it unto me.

28 He hath redeemed me from passing to corruption,
   And my life, that it should behold the light."

29 Lo! all these things worketh God
   Twice, yea thrice, with man,

30 To withhold him from corruption,
   That He may be enlightened with the light of life.

31 Attend, O Job, hearken unto Me,
   Keep silence, and I Myself will speak.

32 If thou hast words, refute Me;
   Speak, for I desire that thou shouldest be justified.

33 If not, do thou hearken unto Me,
   Keep silence, and I will teach thee wisdom.

CHAPTER XXXIV.

1 Then responded Elihu, and said :

2 Hear My words, ye wise men,
  And hearken unto Me, ye men of discernment.

3 For the ear proveth words,
  Even as the palate tasteth meat.

4 Let us choose for ourselves what is right,
  Let us discern among ourselves what is good.

5 For Job hath said : "I am righteous,
  And God hath deprived me of my right.

6 In respect to my right I am regarded as a liar ;
  The arrow within me is fatal, though I have not apostatized."

7 What man is there like unto Job,
  Who drinketh in scoffing like water ?

8 And travelleth in company with workers of iniquity,
  Even to journey with wicked men ?

9 For he hath said : " A man profiteth nothing
  By delighting himself in God."

10 Therefore, ye men of understanding, hearken unto Me,
  Far be it from God to do wickedly,
  And from the Almighty to act iniquitously.

11 For according to a man's work will He requite to him,
  And according to a man's way it shall befall him.

12 Surely of a truth God will not do wickedly,
  Nor will the Almighty pervert justice.

13 Who hath committed to Him the supervision of the earth ?
  Yea, who hath disposed the whole habitable globe ?

14 Should He (God) severely scrutinize him (man),
  He would recall to Himself his spirit and his breath.

15 All flesh would expire together,
  And man would return to dust.

16 If then thou hast understanding, hear thou this,
  Give ear to the sound of My words.

17 Shall He reign that hateth right ?
  Yea, wilt thou condemn the Just Supreme ?

18 Existeth there any one who saith to a king, " Thou art Belial,"
  Or to princes, " Ye are iniquity ?"

19 How less to Him, who regardeth not the person of princes,
   Nor notices the affluent more than the poor,
   For they are all the workmanship of His hands.

20 In a moment they die, yea, at midnight,
   The people tremble and pass away,
   And the mighty man is removed without hand.

21 For His eyes are on the ways of man,
   And he surveyeth all his footsteps.

22 There is no darkness and no death-shade,
   Where the workers of iniquity can shroud themselves.

23 For He hath laid no more upon man than this,
   That he must come to God to judgment.

24 He crusheth the mighty without inquisition,
   And raiseth up others in their stead.

25 For He taketh cognizance of their actions,
   And He turneth night upon them, and they are crushed.

26 Because they are wicked, He smiteth them,
   In the presence of beholders.

27 Because they turned away from after Him,
   And regarded none of His ways,

28 So as to make the cry of the destitute to come before Him,
   And that He should hear the cry of the oppressed.

29 When He giveth peace, who can make trouble?
   When He hideth His face, who then shall behold Him?
   And this in respect to a nation and to an individual alike.

30 That the profane man no more bear rule,
   That the people be no more ensnared,

31 Surely to God it should be said:
   "I have borne sin, I will not act perversely.

32 Beyond what I see teach Thou me;
   If I have done iniquity, I will do it no more."

33 Hath He requited thee of thine own, though thou rejectest?
   Thou must indeed determine, and not I:
   Therefore speak what thou knowest.

34 Men of understanding will say to me,
    Even the wise man who heareth me :
35 " Job hath spoken without knowledge,
    And his words have been without discretion."
36 My desire is, that Job may thoroughly be tried,
    Because his answers resemble those of wicked men.
37 For he addeth unto his sin,
    In our presence he applaudeth transgression,
    And multiplieth his words against God.

CHAPTER XXXV.

1 Then responded Elihu, and said :

2 Deemest thou this to be right ?
    Thou hast said : " I am more just than God."

3 For thou hast said : " What shall I profit in respect to thee ?
    And how shall I be advantaged more than by my sin ?"

4 I myself will reply to thine arguments,
    And to those of thy friends with thee.

5 Look up unto the heavens, and behold,
    Contemplate also the clouds, which are high above thee.

6 If thou hast sinned, what effectest thou against Him ?
    And if thy transgressions be multiplied, what doest thou unto Him ?

7 If thou art righteous, what givest thou unto Him ?
    Or what will He receive from thy hand ?

8 Thy wickedness affecteth a man like thyself,
    And thy righteousness a child of man.

9 Because of the multitude of oppressions, men cry out,
    Because of the arm of the mighty they cry aloud.

10 But none saith : " Where is God, my Maker ?
    Who giveth songs in the night ?

11 Who teacheth us more than the beasts of the earth,
    And maketh us wiser than the birds of heaven ?"

12 Then they cry aloud, but He answereth not,
Because of the pride of evil men.

13 Surely God will not listen to vanity,
Nor will the Almighty regard it.

14 Although thou sayest, thou canst not see Him ;
Justice is with Him, therefore wait thou for Him.

15 But now because His anger visits not,
And He taketh not severe vengeance of thy arrogance,

16 Therefore doth Job open his mouth in vanity,
He multiplieth words without knowledge.

CHAPTER XXXVI.

1 Then resumed ELIHU, and said :

2 Bear with Me a little, and I will show thee
That there are yet arguments on behalf of God.

3 I will bring My knowledge from afar,
And will ascribe righteousness to My Maker.

4 For truly My words are no falsehood,
Perfect in knowledge (I stand) before thee.

5 Lo ! God is almighty, and will not be despised,
Almighty in strength of understanding.

6 He will not prosper the evil-doer,
And will render justice to the oppressed.

7 He withholdeth not His eyes from him that is righteous,
But (will place him) with kings on a throne,
And will cause them to sit for ever, and they shall be exalted.

8 And when men, bound with chains,
Are held in bonds of affliction,

9 He thereby showeth to them their work,
And their transgressions, that they have acted arrogantly ;

10 And openeth their ears to correction,
And commandeth that they return from iniquity.

11 If they shall hearken and serve Him,
   They shall complete their days in prosperity,
   And their years in pleasures.

12 But if they shall not hearken,
   With the dart they shall pass away,
   And shall expire without knowledge.

13 Thus the profane in heart treasure up wrath,
   They cry not (to God) when He bindeth them.

14 Their existence shall expire in childishness,
   Though their life have been spent with the saints.

15 He delivereth the afflicted in his affliction,
   And by oppression openeth their ear.

16 And thee would He have turned from the gorge of distress,
   A broad place without straitness should have been substituted for it,
   And the provision of thy table should have been full of fat.

17 But thou hast fully advocated an irreligious cause,
   The cause and the judgment thereon arraign thee.

18 Wherefore (beware) lest anger stir thee up against chastisement,
   Then a great ransom cannot deliver thee.

19 Will He value thy boundless affluence?
   Or all the munitions of power?

20 Long not for the night (of death)
   But for the ascending of the peoples from their abode below.

21 Take heed, turn not thou aside to transgression,
   For this thou hast chosen rather than affliction.

22 Behold, God manifests His greatness by His power;
   Who is Lord like unto Him?

23 Remember that thou magnify His work,
   Which men in song extol.

24 All the Adamic race gaze thereon,
   Man contemplates it from afar.

(GOD'S OMNIPOTENCE.)

26 Lo! God is great, therefore we cannot know Him,
   (Great also is) the number of His years, therefore it is unsearchable.

27 For He evaporates the water-drops
   Which are fused into rain by means of His vapour,

28 Which (rain) the clouds pour down,
   They distil upon man abundantly.

(LIGHTNING, THUNDER, STORM, AND WHIRLWIND.)

29 Who indeed can understand the expansion of the clouds,
   The loud-sounding tempests of His pavilion?

30 Lo! around it He outspreads His light,
   And (therewith) covers the ocean-depths.

31 For by them He executeth judgments upon the peoples,
   By them He giveth food abundantly.

32 Lightning covers the vaulted skies,
   And He charges it where to strike.

33 His thunder proclaims concerning Him
   Possession of wrath against iniquity.

CHAPTER XXXVII.

1 Yea, at this my heart palpitates,
  And leapeth from its place.

2 Hearken attentively to the roar of His thunder,
  And the rumbling which proceedeth from His mouth.

3 Beneath the whole heavens He directs it,
  And His lightning to the ends of the earth.

4 After it the thunder roareth,
  He thunders with His majestic voice,
  And none can trace them, though His voice is heard.

5 God thunders marvellously with His voice,
  Great things doeth He, which we cannot comprehend.

6 Behold! He proclaimeth to the snow: "Be thou;"
   To the earth, and there is a downfall of rain,
   Yea, a downfall of the drenching rains of His might.

7 The handywork of every man sealeth He up,
   That all men may acknowledge His workmanship.

8 Then the wild beasts go into covert,
   And in their dens abide.

9 From the unseen (South) issues the whirlwind,
   And from the distant (poles) the cold.

10 By the breath of God ice is given,
   And the expanse of the waters is compressed.

11 Yea, for irrigation He stretches out the thick cloud,
   His lightning disperses the cloudy vapour.

12 And He by His counsels continuously changeth their evolutions,
   That they may do whatsoever He commandeth them,
   On the face of the habitable globe, upon the whole earth,

13 Whether truly for a scourge upon His earth,
   Or for mercy He allots it.

14 Give ear to this, O Job;
   Be still, and ponder the wonderful works of God.

15 Dost thou know how God ordaineth these,
   And causeth His lightning-cloud to shine?

16 Dost thou understand the poising of the clouds,
   The wondrous works of Him who is perfect in all knowledge?

17 How thy garments are heated,
   When He attempers the earth by the south wind?

18 Didst thou with Him spread out the heavens,
   Unyielding as a molten mirror?

19 Inform us what we shall say unto Him,
   Unto Him arrayed in robes of darkness.

20 Shall it be told Him that I am speaking?
   Should a man speak, he would infallibly be consumed.

21 But now men eye not the light,
    When it is shining in the skies,
    And the wind passeth over, and cleareth them.

22 Out of the North radiates the golden light ;
    With God there is terrible majesty.

23 The Almighty ! we cannot find Him out ;
    Great in power, and rectitude, and plenitude of justice,
    He will never oppress.

24 Therefore let men fear Him
    Whom none of the wise of heart have ever seen.

CHAPS. XXXII.-XXXVII. ELIHU.—The writers on the Book of Job, almost without one exception, consider ELIHU to have been a mere mortal, a man of like passions with themselves, born in sin and conceived in iniquity. Hence many do not hesitate to impute to ELIHU defect of language, inconclusiveness of argument, caustic severity of judgment, misquotation of the words and sentiments of Job, even wilful misrepresentation and actual falsehood. Now, if Elihu was, what I believe him to have been, the Son of God appearing to Job, Eliphaz, Bildad, and Zophar in human form, then this language is (however unconscious and undesigned) blasphemy against the only name under heaven given among men whereby they can be saved. Well does Bishop Wordsworth argue : "Elihu limited his expostulations with Job to TWO POINTS. He remonstrated with him for trying to justify himself before God, and for regarding God as his enemy, on account of his present sufferings. In these TWO POINTS, the Sacred Writer himself sides with Elihu. If therefore we were to censure Elihu in these two respects (as some have done), we should censure God Himself." I contend that what Melchizedek was to Abraham, Elihu was unto Job, the manifestation of the Second Person of the Trinity in the form of man, a prelibation of His incarnation. I deduce this inference—I. From the Names ; II. From the Acts ; III. From the Descriptions of Melchizedek and Elihu.

I. Melchizedek signifies the King of Righteousness, which name is indicative of Messiah's divine and perfect righteousness, which is unto and upon all them that believe, for justification before a heart-searching God. He is also King of Salem ; that is, King of Peace, because they who are justified by faith have peace with God through Christ. Rosenmüller interprets Elihu, MY GOD IS THE TRUE GOD, and MY GOD IS JEHOVAH. The writer of the Book of Job, by this appellation and by the descriptive words which follow, namely,—MY GOD JEHOVAH, THE BLESSED SON OF GOD, THE DESPISED ONE, manifestly implies, that ELIHU was God in the form of man.

II. Melchizedek met Abraham returning from the slaughter of the kings, and brought forth bread and wine, prelibations of sacramental bread and wine, by the reception of which believers are commanded to show forth Christ's death until He shall come. Melchizedek also blessed Abraham. Now the less is blessed of the greater. Can any one, except the Son of God, be greater than the Father of the faithful and the Friend of God ? ELIHU is declared to be, THE BLESSED SON OF GOD, THE DESPISED ONE, OF THE LINEAGE OF THE MOST HIGH. He asserts His possession of perfection of knowledge, and speaks oracularly as infallible. These appellations and these perfections are verified in Immanuel, and in Immanuel alone.

III. Melchizedek is divinely described to be " without father, without mother, without descent, having neither beginning of days, nor end of life " (*Hebrews* vii. 3). Can this be predicated of any mere mortal man ? Can it be predicated of any one but of Him, whose goings forth have been from everlasting, whose incarnation was by the overshadowing of the Holy Ghost, who is, and was, and is to come, the Almighty ? Melchizedek abideth a priest for ever, in contradistinction to priests of mankind, who follow each other in continuous succession. Job testifies of Elihu : " I have heard of Thee by the hearing of the ear, but now mine eye seeth Thee." Job could not have seen the plenitude of Jehovah's glory veiled from his sight by the intervention of the whirlwind. " No man hath seen God at any time " (1 *John* iv. 12). But He whom Job saw was " the actual manifestation of the Son of God, who appeared in the anticipated form of man, which he often assumed before His incarnation" (*Biddulph*), "the brightness of His Father's glory, and the express image of His person,"—the Manifester of God's glory to man. ELIHU asserts this of Himself: "I am, according to thy wish, IN THE PLACE OF GOD."—xxxiii. 6.

To this statement it has been objected, that the appearance of Messiah under the form of man previous to His incarnation would be self-contradictory. The reply to this objection is, that such appearances are recorded in Scripture, and that two at least of these appearances admit of no denial. Three men appeared to Abraham in the plains of Mamre. One of these is called JEHOVAH, the incommunicable name of the one living and true God. Jehovah converses with Abraham, foretells to him the approaching conflagration of the Pentapolis, and hears and answers his prayers. This Jehovah must have been Messiah in human form. Again, at the brook Jabbok, "a man wrestled with Jacob until the breaking of the day." On this transaction Jacob remarks, "I have seen God face to face, and my life is preserved." This man must have been Messiah in human form.

Kind friends have forewarned me of the rancorous hostility this volume will experience on account of this Messianic interpretation. That their anticipations will be realized I doubt not. But honesty forbids the suppression of what I believe to be scriptural truth. I dare not keep back what I believe to be the will of God; and, if His will, profitable to man. Duty to God and man impels me to record my own convictions, without addition or subtraction, of what God hath revealed in the Book of Job, whether men will hear, or whether they will forbear. Magna est veritas, et prevalebit.

The Hebrew original of xxxii. 2 and 6 verses is ambiguous, and is capable of a twofold interpretation; of that of our Authorized Version derived from the ancient versions, and of the translation I have appended thereto. To the translation so appended it may be objected, that the verb ברך lacks the ן, which is the formative of the Pahul participle. To this objection the reply is twofold: 1. That the addition of the human masoretic punctuation to God's inspired original has caused so many irregularities and anomalies in the *matres lectionis*, that the absence of any one of the *matres lectionis* (the omission of which may be compensated by the insertion of a point) is of common occurrence; 2. That in 2 Samuel ii. 5 the ן is similarly deficient in the Pahul participle of ברך. To the Authorized Version it may reasonably be objected, that whilst Job, Eliphaz, Bildad, and Zophar are described by their respective abodes at Uz, Teman, Shuah, and Naama, Elihu is designated as the scion of an unknown father, family, and tribe—who takes part in the argument without introduction—who leaves without reply, commendation, or censure—and whose discourse is manifestly the exordium, and an integral portion, of the speech of Jehovah from the whirlwind. "Elihu's argument is followed up, adopted, and continued by God Himself speaking out of the whirlwind. The voice of Elihu dies away in the thunders of Jehovah."—*Bishop Wordsworth.*

Froude admits that the critics of Germany, who reject the Divinity of Elihu, reject also the genuineness of the speech attributed to him. "The speech of Elihu, which lies between Job's last words, and God's appearance, is now decisively pronounced by Hebrew scholars not to be genuine. The most superficial reader will have been perplexed by the introduction of a speaker, to whom no allusion is made, either in the prologue or the epilogue." This criticism is self-consistent. Misinterpretation or rejection of the speech of Elihu is the necessary consequent of the denial of Elihu to be the manifestation of Messiah in the anticipated form of man. The Messiahship of Elihu, and a just appreciation of His speech to Job, must stand or fall together.

VER. 21.—The rendering of this verse in the Coptic Version is very peculiar:—

"For I will not be ashamed before man,
Neither will I be confounded before one born of woman."

CHAP. XXXIII. VER. 19-28.—In verses 19-22, ELIHU describes the loathsome and emaciating disease of elephantiasis with which Job was afflicted, in verses 23 and 24 He declares His Mediatorship and Intercession on his behalf, and in verses 25-28 He predicts Job's restoration to health, prosperity, and heart-communion with his covenant-God.

VER. 23.—There are three interpretations of this verse: One interpretation represents the Person described as "one above a thousand," to be a mere man, whose official duty it is to impart Divine truth to his fellow-creatures. The second interpretation depicts him as an angel. The third interpretation declares Him to be the one Mediator between God and man, the second Person of the eternal Trinity. The first interpretation cannot be correct, because no mortal can say, "I have found a ransom or an atonement." "None can by any means redeem his brother, nor give to God a ransom for him" (*Psalm* xlix. 7). The second interpretation cannot stand, because the office of the elect angels is to "minister to them that are heirs of salvation," not to ransom them, not to atone for them, not to save them in whole or in part. The third interpretation is the only key which can unlock this passage. This interpretation exhibits to us the predicted Messiah manifest in human form, a prelibation of His incarnation—the angel of the everlasting covenant—the only Mediator between God and man—most excellent and infinitely supreme above all created beings—who alone can impart to the believer His righteousness for justification—who is the only ransom and atonement for fallen sinful man.

In this 23d verse ELIHU states His own attributes, perfections, and offices towards all whom He hath redeemed, and justified, and sanctified, namely, that He is the only-begotten and well-beloved Son, Co-equal, and Servant of the Father, in whom He is well-pleased—the Angel of His presence—the one Intercessor between a holy God and an apostate world—infinitely pure, sinless, and impeccable—whose righteousness received by faith is the justification of all that are saved—the wisdom, righteousness, sanctification, and redemption, the prophet, priest, and king of all, to whom Elihu the righteous Judge and King will say: "Come, ye blessed of my Father, inherit the kingdom prepared for you from the foundation of the world" (*Matthew* xxv. 32). Bishop Wordsworth has remarked, that some of the Rabbis themselves have applied this verse to the Messiah, and that Schultetus, Schultens, and other writers regard these words as spoken by Christ. The Bishop adds, "The sense is virtually the same. God gave His own Son for us all (Romans viii. 32), and the Son of Man came to give His life a RANSOM for many (Matthew xx. 28), Christ gave himself as a RANSOM for all (1 Timothy ii. 6)."

VER. 23. *A Mediator.*—Genesis xlii. 23 fully explains the meaning of this word. It there signifies an officer of the Egyptian court, whose official function was not so much to interpret to Joseph the language of the foreigners who came down to Egypt to buy corn, but rather to convey to Joseph their petitions, and to communicate to them Joseph's official replies. This officer of state, without whose intervention there was no access to Joseph, Governor of Egypt, was a fit emblem of Him who is the one Mediator between God and man, who ever liveth to make intercession for His people, to present their prayers to God for acceptance, and to make known to them by the Spirit God's answer to their prayers, and His Divine will concerning them.—*See* Parkhurst's *Hebrew Lexicon*, Schultens *on Job*, and Dr. Hodge's *Elihu.*

VER. 23. *One above a thousand.*—Schultens interprets these words to signify THE MOST EXCELLENT ONE. "Mihi nil simplicius, quam, UNUS E MILLE pro EXCELLENTISSIMUS."

VER. 24. *Then shall He be gracious unto him.*—THEN, after that Messiah shall have revealed to man Himself as the only law-fulfiller, and shall have impressed upon his heart, that His Divine righteousness, received by faith, is the only method of man's justification in the sight of God, Messiah will be gracious unto him, and will say, " I have found a ransom."

VER. 26. *His righteousness.*—Schultens considers these words to signify peace with God and boldness of access by the spirit of adoption to Christ and the throne of grace, which peace Job had lost for a time from the buffetings of Satan, and his mental and bodily depression. "He will restore to man in Christ, the second Adam, that righteousness which man lost by the fall of the first Adam. The word for MAN here is ENOSH, *i.e.*, man in his weakness and corruption, to which he was reduced by the fall."—*Bishop Wordsworth.*

VER. 27.—The Coptic Version renders most happily the last hemistich of this verse: "He hath not afflicted me according to the desert of the sins which I have committed."

VER. 29. *Twice, yea thrice.*—The Authorized Version correctly renders this Hebrew idiomatic phrase by OFTENTIMES.

CHAP. XXXV. VER. 2. *I am more just than God.*—Literally, "My just cause is more than the just cause of God."

CHAP. XXXVI. VER. 7. *With kings on a throne.*—This millennial glory will be consummated at the Second Advent, when the saints, sole partakers of the first resurrection, shall take the kingdom, and possess the kingdom for ever, as predicted by John in the Apocalypse. (Christ) "hath made us kings and priests unto God His Father" (i. 6). (Christ) "hath made us unto our God kings and priests, and we shall reign ON THE EARTH" (v. 10). "They who have part in the first resurrection shall be priests of God and of Christ, and shall reign with Him a thousand years" (xx. 6).

VER. 12. *With the dart they shall pass away.* "Like an arrow that cutteth the air, and leaves no trace behind, so they pass by, and die without being known or remembered."—*Fry.*

Ver. 13. *He bindeth them.*—That is, with bonds of affliction, named in verse 8.

Ver. 14. *Childishness.*—Childish ignorance of God, of His revealed will, of the way of salvation, and of the promised seed of the woman.—*See* Parkhurst's *Hebrew Lexicon*, who vindicates this interpretation of the word, and refers to Isaiah iii. 4; Ecclesiastes x. 16, 17; and 2 Chronicles xiii. 7. See also Proverbs xxii. 15.

With the saints.—If the usual interpretation be adhered to, it will follow, that the sin of Sodom, resulting from polytheism, was practised in the age and vicinity of Job. There is no other reference in the Book of Job either to this sin or to any idolatry except Sabæism, or the worship of the sun and moon; however, idolatry, and the worship of Venus, with all its attendant impurities, may have existed in Chaldæa, in Egypt, and in other countries.

Ver. 20.—" This verse is spoken in reproof of the eager desire which Job had several times expressed for his death—Long not for the night of death—that ' night when no man can work.' Let not this be the object of desire, but rather long for the resurrection of the dead, when the dead shall leave their unknown abodes in the regions below. This is consonant with the general instructions of the Word of God. That which is held forth as the great object of the believer's hope; for which, as the expression implies, they may ' pant with desire,' and with the expectation of which they may comfort one another in all the seasons of their toil and trouble, is not so much the day of their death, but the ' day of the Lord,' when they that sleep in Christ shall come forth to the better resurrection."—*Fry.*

Ver. 21. *Transgression.*—Rebellion of thy will against God's will, dissatisfaction with God's providential administration of the universe, defect of implicit submission to God, supreme Arbiter of human affairs. The defect of Job's faith and obedience was his inability to say from his heart: "Not my will, but Thine, be done." Yet how severely was Job tried! How few of God's children, even under the full meridian blaze of Gospel light, with all their superiority of light, and knowledge, and experience, if similarly circumstanced as Job was, would have spoken and acted better than Job did!

Chap. xxxvii. Ver. 6.—The difficulty of this verse, evidenced by the multitudinous interpretations thereof, arises from the absence of a preposition to govern the Hebrew noun rendered earth. The Hebrew, literally translated, would be, " be thou earth." But by arranging this verse as a triplet, and by construing the Hebrew nouns translated snow and earth as dative cases governed by the same preposition, the preposition prefixed to the Hebrew noun translated snow would be understood before the Hebrew noun translated earth, in perfect accordance with the idiom of the Hebrew language.

Ver. 16. *The poising of the clouds.*—" The clouds, which seem to be driven about capriciously and at random, at the mercy of fierce winds, or to be ready to burst with torrents and cataracts of water, are all suspended in the air, and are weighed in a balance by God."—*Bishop Wordsworth.*

Ver. 19. *Unto Him arrayed in robes of darkness.*—This is the version of Reiske and Mason Good.—*See* Mason Good, page 440, who explains and vindicates this version.

Ver. 20. This verse intimates plainly that Elihu was more than man. Elihu speaks in full security, but He declares that should a man speak, he would infallibly be consumed. Hence Elihu, by His own declaration, was more than man.

Ver. 21-23.—As the human eye cannot gaze on the meridian brightness of the full-orbed sun, so the human mind cannot comprehend the plenitude of God's glory and majesty. This is beautifully expressed in Scott's metrical version of these three verses:—

> " When heaven's expanse the sweeping north-wind clears,
> And, flaming forth, the golden sun appears,
> Whose optic on the dazzling scene can gaze?
> How, then, abide a God's terrific blaze?
> In vain we pry, in vain our reason toils,
> Immensity the force of reason foils:
> Justice and boundless power exalt His throne,
> Beneficent to all, unjust to none."

See the translations of Schultens, Rosenmüller, Dathe, and Lee, which substantially accord with Scott's interpretation of this sublime poetic imagery.

FIRST ADDRESS OF JEHOVAH TO JOB.

CHAPTERS XXXVIII., XXXIX., XL., AND XLI.

Jehovah addresses His speech solely and exclusively to Job—reproves the Patriarch for having spoken presumptuously of the Providential administration of the world, far above his knowledge and comprehension—and asserts His Sovereignty as Creator, Preserver, Administrator, and Governor of the universe, and of all that is therein, having a right to do as He will with His own.

1 Then Jehovah answered Job
   Out of the whirlwind, and said :

2 Who is this that darkeneth counsel
   By words without knowledge ?

3 Gird up now thy loins like a man,
   And I will question thee, and inform thou Me.

(CREATION.)

4 Where wast thou when I laid the foundations of the earth ?
   Declare, if thou intelligently knowest.

5 Who fixed its measurements ? For thou knowest.
   Or who hath stretched the plumb-line over it ?

6 On what were its foundations sunken ?
   Or who hath laid its corner-stone ?

(THE DELUGE.)

7 (Where wast thou) when the morning stars sang together,
   And all the sons of God rejoiced triumphantly,

8 And the sea was pent up with doors,
   After its gush from the womb had overflowed.

9 And I made the clouds its mantle,
   And thick darkness its swaddling-bands.

10 And I appointed to it My boundary,
    And ordained bars and doors.

11 And I said : "Thus far shalt thou come, and no further ;
    And here shall thy proud waves be stayed."

(MORNING-LIGHT.)
12 Hast thou, within thy days, ordained the orient morn;
   Hast thou assigned to the day-spring its place;
13 That it should embrace the extremities of the earth,
   And that evil-doers should be terrified thereby?
14 It (the earth) is transformed as clay by the signet-ring,
   And (its extremities) stand forth as in a robe of light.
15 But from evil-doers their light is withdrawn,
   And the uplifted arm is shivered.

(THE OCEAN.)
16 Hast thou penetrated to the fountains of the ocean?
   And hast thou journeyed to explore the deep?

(DEATH.)
17 Have the gates of death been disclosed to thee?
   And hast thou beheld the gates of the death-shade?

(THE EARTH.)
18 Hast thou surveyed earth's wide expanded bounds?
   Declare the whole thereof, if thou knowest.

(LIGHT AND DARKNESS.)
19 Which is the road to where light dwelleth?
   And darkness, where is its abode?
20 Verily thou canst conduct us to its boundary,
   Yea, verily, thou discernest the paths to its mansion.
21 Thou knowest, because thou wast then born,
   And the number of thy days is great.

(SNOW, HAIL, RAIN, ICE, FROST.)
22 Hast thou entered into the stores of snow,
   And hast thou beheld the stores of hail,
23 Which I have reserved for the time of tribulation,
   For the day of conflict and battle?
24 Which is the road to whence forks the lightning-flash?
   (Which is the road to) whence the Eastern levanter bursts over the earth?

25 Who hath apportioned to the water-spout its course?
  And to the thunder-flash its pathway?
26 To cause rain to fall on a land where there is no man,
  On a desert wherein there is no mortal;
27 To saturate the waste and the wilderness,
  And to make the springing herbage to grow.
28 Hath the rain a father?
  Or who hath begotten the globules of the dew?
29 Out of whose womb came the ice?
  And the hoar-frost of heaven, who hath engendered it?
30 Stone-like the waters are hidden,
  And the surfaces of the deep are congealed.

(THE CONSTELLATIONS AND CELESTIAL PHENOMENA.)

31 Canst thou withhold the delights of Cimah (the vernal constellation)?
  Or relax the contractions of Cesil (the brumal constellation)?
32 Canst thou bring forth Mazzaroth in his season?
  Or canst thou guide Ash (the circling polar star) and his (stellar) attendants?
33 Understandest thou the ordinances of the heavens?
  Or hast thou appointed to each its dominion over the earth?
34 Canst thou lift up thy voice to the clouds?
  So that deluges of water shall envelop thee.
35 Canst thou send forth the lightnings, so that they shall go,
  And shall say unto thee: "Here we are?"
36 Who supplieth wisdom to the darting flashes?
  And who imparteth intelligence to the meteors?
37 Who by wisdom can irradiate the skies?
  And who can empty the bottles of heaven,
38 When the dust is compressed into hardness,
  And the clods cohere together?

(THE LION.)

39 Canst thou hunt down prey for the lioness?
  Or satisfy the appetite of the young lions

40 When they crouch down in their lairs—
   Lie in ambush in the covert?

(THE RAVEN.)
41 Who provides for the raven its prey
   When its young ones cry unto God,
   (When) they wander for lack of food?

CHAPTER XXXIX.

(THE IBEX OR ROCK-GOAT.)
1 Knowest thou the time when the rock-goats bring forth?
   Canst thou observe the parturition of the hinds?
2 Canst thou reckon the months they fulfil?
   And dost thou know the season when they bring forth?
3 (When) they couch down, they eject their young?
   (When) they cast off their labour-pains?
4 (When) their young ones mature their strength, herd on the plain,
   Go forth, and return to them no more?

(THE WILD ASS.)
5 Who hath sent out the wild ass (to roam) at large?
   And who hath loosed the brayer's bands?
6 Whose house I have made the wilderness,
   And his haunts the salt waste.
7 He scorneth the tumult of the city:
   The shouts of the driver he regardeth not.
8 He traverseth the mountains, his pasturage,
   And he searcheth after every green thing.

(THE PRIMEVAL WILD OX, OR WILD OX OF YORE.)
9 Will the wild ox be willing to serve thee?
   Will he abide through the night at thy crib?
10 Canst thou confine the wild ox to the furrow by his rope?
   Will he harrow the valleys after thee?
11 Canst thou confide in him, because his strength is great,
   And commit unto him the product of thy labour?

12 Wilt thou trust him that he will bring home thy grain ?
   And ingather it on thy threshing-floor ?

(THE OSTRICH.)

13 The wing of the ostrich-tribe flaps exultingly,
   Truly they have goodly pinion and plumage.

14 Lo ! she commits her eggs to the earth,
   And leaveth them to be warmed in the sand ;

15 And forgetteth that the foot may crush them,
   And that the wild beast may trample upon them.

16 She is hardened against her young, as if they were not her own ;
   Vain is her travail, being without solicitude.

17 For God hath made her oblivious of wisdom,
   And hath not imparted to her understanding.

18 What time erect she speeds her course,
   She laugheth at the horse and his rider.

(THE WAR HORSE.)

19 Hast thou given strength to the horse ?
   Hast thou clothed his neck with the thunder-flash ?

20 Hast thou made him to bound like the locust ?
   His proud snorting is terrible.

21 They paw the valley, and he exulteth in strength,
   He rusheth forth to meet the clashing host.

22 He mocketh at fear, and is undismayed ;
   Neither turneth he aside from the edge of the sword.

23 Against him rattleth the quiver,
   The glittering spear, and the lance.

24 With trembling and rage he swallows the ground,
   And will no longer stand still when the trumpet hath sounded.

25 With the blast of the trumpet he saith : Ah, ah !
   And scents the battle from afar.
   The war-cry of the chieftains, and the battle-shout.

(The Hawk.)

26 Doth the hawk take wing by thy instruction?
  And spread out his pinions southwards?

(The Eagle.)

27 Is it at thy command that the eagle soars aloft,
  And that he makes his nest on high?

28 He inhabits the rock, and lodgeth
  Upon the crag of the rock, even upon his mountain-citadel.

29 From thence he espieth his prey,
  His eyes discern it from afar.

30 Yea, his nestlings gulp down the blood,
  And where the slain are there is he.

CHAPTER XL.

(The Crocodile.)

15 Behold now behemoth, which I have created,
  Will he eat grass with thee like the herd?

16 Behold now his strength is in his loins,
  And his vigour in the muscles of his belly.

17 He brandisheth his tail. He resembles the cedar of Lebanon,
  The sinews of his thighs are interlaced together.

18 His bones are as tubes of brass,
  His large bones are as forged bars of iron.

19 He is the chief of the ways of God,
  His Maker has made fast his weapons.

20 For did the mountains yield him food,
  There all the wild beasts of the field would be slaughtered.

21 Beneath shady trees he coucheth,
  In the covert of reeds and the ooze.

22 The shady trees conceal him with their shadow,
  The osiers of the river encompass him.

23 Should the river impetuously overflow, he is not startled,
  He is unmoved though Jordan rush against his mouth.

24 On his eyes would he receive it,
   His snout would cut through the roaring waves.

CHAPTER XLI.

1 Canst thou draw out leviathan with a hook?
  And bind his tongue with a cord?

2 Canst thou pass a rush-cord through his snout?
  Or perforate his jaw with a ring?

3 Will he make many supplications unto thee?
  Will he speak soft words unto thee?

4 Will he make a covenant with thee?
  Canst thou take him to be thy servant for ever?

5 Canst thou sport with him as with a bird?
  Yea, wilt thou encage him for thy maidens?

6 Shall confederates delve for him a pitfall?
  Shall they part him among the merchants?

7 Canst thou fill his skin with harpoons?
  And his head with fish-spears?

8 Lay thine hand upon him,
  Be mindful of the conflict. Thou shalt never essay it again.

9 Behold, the hope of (taking) him is fallacious;
  Is it not dissipated by the very sight of him?

10 None is so foolhardy as to rouse him up;
   Who then is he that arrayeth himself against Me?

11 Who has first given Me that I should repay?
   All under the whole heaven is mine.

12 But I will not be silent concerning his powers,
   The relation of his might, and the destructiveness of his armature.

13 Who has uncovered his mailed face?
   Who can contend against his double jaws?

14 Who can open the valves of his face?
   The rows of his teeth are terrific.

15 Magnificent are the bosses of (his) shields,
   Soldered together with a close seal.

16 They are compacted one to another,
   So that no air can penetrate between them;

17 They are fastened each to its fellow,
   They adhere together, and cannot be sundered.

18 His sneezings irradiate light,
   And his eyes resemble the glancings of the dawn.

19 From his mouth issue flames,
   Sparks of fire dart forth.

20 From his nostrils proceedeth smoke,
   As from a seething pot, or a caldron.

21 His breath enkindles coals,
   And flame bursts forth from his mouth.

22 In his neck dwelleth MIGHT,
   And TERROR bounds before him.

23 The tendons of his flesh are soldered together,
   Each is firm upon him, and cannot be moved.

24 His heart is firm as a very stone,
   Yea, as firm as the nether millstone.

25 At his rising up the mighty are afraid,
   At (his) breakings forth they betake themselves to flight.

26 The sword of him that attacks him cannot hold,
   Nor the spear, the dart, or the lance.

27 Iron he accounteth as straw.
   Brass as rotten wood.

28 The arrow cannot make him flee.
   The sling stones against him are turned into stubble.

29 Clubs are accounted as stubble,
   And he laugheth at the brandishing of a spear.

30 His bed is sharp splinters,
   Which the broken rock scattereth on the mud.

31 He maketh the deep to boil like a caldron;
   He maketh the sea odoriferous as perfume.

32 Behind him he maketh a shining pathway,
   One would think the deep to be hoary.

33 There is not upon earth his like,
   This creature without fear.

34 He looketh down on all that are exalted,—
   He the king over all the sons of pride.

CHAP. XXXVIII. VER. 1. *Out of the whirlwind.*—"The Book of Job records and makes known a most wonderful miracle, the Voice from heaven, that God had spoken magnificently, solemnly, as He spake from Mount Sinai; and again at the baptism of our Lord, at His transfiguration, at His manifestation to the Greek strangers, at His final entry into Jerusalem. When the Lord had spoken to Adam and Eve and to Abraham, it appears to have been to them alone. His voice out of the whirlwind was the first heard openly and with witnesses. Was not this the great Patriarchal revelation, as that at Sinai was the Mosaic?"—*Mazzaroth*, by Miss Rolleston.

VER. 15. *Their light.*—Evil-doers change day into night, and night into day, secreting themselves by day, and by night being active in evil. Hence darkness is to them light, and light is darkness. See Chapter xxiv. 13 and 16. Therefore THEIR LIGHT, by poetic license, signifies in this verse THEIR NIGHT, which is terminated by sun-rising, whereby their deeds of violence are checked, and their arm shivered. "Nox impiis idem est quod dies bonis. Illa IMPIORUM DIES ad lucis ortum præterit; jam abstinere debent ab operibus suis."—*Dathe.* See also *Rosenmüller.*

VER. 21. *Days.*—That is, YEARS. The Hebrew language has a proper noun for YEARS. But instead thereof the word DAYS, which occasionally has the definite signification of YEARS, seems here to be advisedly employed to intimate the recent creation of Job, and the brevity of his life, as compared with the creation of light and darkness.

VER. 30. The imagery of this verse is most beautiful and most correct. The fluidity of water is hidden or concealed from sight, the surface thereof being congealed by frost, whereby it becomes STONE-LIKE, both opaque and hard.

VERS. 31-33.—"The Divine voice named Cimah and Cesil, Ash and Mazzaroth, as things that are, but beyond the reach of man, subject to the Creator's will. These are not the astronomy of Job, they are the astronomy of revelation. The same voice speaks of the 'ordinances of heaven,' 'the dominion thereof upon the earth.' Was there not here implied gravitation and motion, the centripetal and centrifugal force?"—*Mazzaroth*, by Miss Rolleston. For explanation of Cimah, Cesil, and Ash see note on ix. 9, p. 28, and Critical Appendix.

VER. 41. *The raven.*—"Of the raven there are eight species found in Palestine. In no country are the species more numerous in individuals. Of all the birds of Jerusalem the raven tribe are the most characteristic and conspicuous, though the larger species is quite outnumbered by its smaller companion. They are present everywhere to eye and ear, and the odours that float around remind us of their use. The raven is a bird of almost world-wide distribution. It is found from Iceland to Japan, through all Asia and Northern Africa, while the ravens of South Africa and the American continent vary very slightly from it, and have often been looked upon as identical."—Tristram's *Natural History.*

CHAP. XXXIX. VER. 1. "The ibex or rock-goat—Hebrew YA'ÉL, that is, the Climber—was well known to the Jews, both in the wilderness and in the Land of Promise itself. Though familiar with the animal, they knew but little of its habits, owing to its extreme wariness and wildness. 'Knowest thou the time when the wild goats of the rock bring forth?' (Job xxxix. 1.) In Arabia Petræa the ibex is very common, generally in small herds of eight or ten individuals."—Tristram's *Natural History.*

VER. 9. *The primeval wild ox.*—"Our translators have unfortunately adopted the rendering of the Septuagint, the 'one-horned' for REEM, which is no fabled monster, but a two-horned reality, a beast which once roamed freely through the forests of Palestine, but now extinct, the AVEROCHS of the old Germans, the URUS of Cæsar, the BOS PRIMIGENIUS of naturalists. Its characteristics are clearly set forth in the passages where the reem (unicorn) is named. The two horns of the reem (unicorn) are the ten thousands of Ephraim, and the thousands of Manasseh, both growing out of ONE head—Joseph. This, then, entirely sets aside the fancy that the rhinoceros, which the Jews could scarcely have known, or any one-horned creature, is intended." "We have evidence of the mighty averochs in Germany down to the Christian æra. The monuments of Assyria represent it among the wild animals chased by the compeers of Semiramis and Sennacherib. Direct evidence was afforded of the former existence of the averochs in Palestine, by our discovery of a mass of bone breccia in the Lebanon, in the flooring of an ancient cave."—Tristram's *Natural History*, p. 146, and his *Land of Israel*, p. 12. Cæsar describes the wild ox of yore as nearly equal to the elephant in size, in form, colour, and figure, resembling the bull, as powerful, swift, savage, and intractable. "Ili sunt magnitudine paullo infra elephantos; specie et colore et figura tauri. Magna vis eorum et magna velocitas; neque homini, neque feræ, quam conspexerint, parcunt. Sed adsuescere ad homines et mansuefieri no parvuli quidem excepti possunt. Amplitudo cornuum et figura et specie multum a nostrorum boum cornubus differt."

VERS. 13-18.—"The speed of the ostrich has been calculated at twenty-six miles an hour by Dr. Livingstone, and yet the South African ostrich is smaller than the Northern species, and I have myself, in the Sahara, measured its stride, when bounding at full speed, from twenty-two to twenty-eight feet. If Dr. Livingstone's calculation be at all correct, the speed of the ostrich is unequalled by any other cursorial animal."—Tristram's *Natural History*. "The ostrich is the largest of existing birds. It usually attains the height of eight feet, but examples have been seen eleven feet in height. One was exhibited in London which took its food from a beam eleven feet from the ground."—Fairbairn's *Bible Dictionary*.

VERS. 19-25.—From a comparison of this highly poetic description of the war-horse with the monumental remains of Egypt, we learn that the first employment of this noble animal was for purposes of war. And as in all Egypt there is only one sculptured representation of an Egyptian rider, and this sculpture of a comparatively recent date (see Wilkinson's *Ancient Egyptians*, vol. i. p. 289), it would seem that the strength of the ancient Oriental armies consisted of war-chariots rather than of cavalry. The Assyrians appear to have been acquainted with the horse at an earlier period than the Egyptians or the Arabians, and to have used the horse indiscriminately for war and for hunting, for the chariot and for the saddle. The eighteenth verse of this chapter proves that horsemen abounded in the vicinity of Job:

"What time erect (the ostrich) speeds her course,
She laugheth at the horse and his rider."

VER. 26.—The Hebrew noun here rendered HAWK, seems a generic name for all the smaller birds of prey, more especially those of migratory habits.

VER. 27.—The Hebrew noun rendered EAGLE, seems to be employed in a generic sense to comprehend all the larger raptorial birds, especially the varied species of eagles and vulturidæ.

CHAP. XL. VER. 17. *Cedar of Lebanon.*—The words, OF LEBANON, are added, because the cedars are now called by the natives of Lebanon by the self-same term by which Job designated them more than 4000 years ago. "The name ARZ is never applied by the natives to any tree but the true cedar."—*See* Tristram's *Land of Israel*, p. 630. "The tail of the crocodile, measured from his haunches, is full half the length of his whole body, and in no other animal whatever, of any very considerable size, is this part so conspicuous, or so meet to be compared to the trunk of a cedar tree."—*Fry*. "Crocodiles propel themselves through the water by the tail, which is also a powerful weapon of attack, and when the beast is captured, a stroke of the tail is more to be dreaded than the teeth. The whole head, back, and tail are covered with quadrangular horny plates or scales, which not only protect the body, a rifle ball glancing off from them as from a rock, but also serve as ballast, enabling the creature to sink rapidly on being disturbed, by merely expelling the air from its lungs."—Tristram's *Natural History*.

CHAP. XLI. VER. 1. *The crocodile.*—Opinions have been, and now are, greatly divided respecting what animals are designated by the Hebrew names BEHEMOTH and LEVIATHAN. The ancients all but universally interpreted LEVIATHAN of the WHALE. This was a manifest error, which is almost now universally exploded. The best modern writers are agreed, that LEVIATHAN designates THE CROCODILE. But respecting BEHEMOTH, great diversity of opinion yet exists. Some consider BEHEMOTH to be the ELEPHANT, some the HIPPOPOTAMOS, some an EXTINCT SAURIAN, and some few have come to the conclusion that BEHEMOTH and LEVIATHAN are two names both designating the CROCODILE. That LEVIATHAN cannot signify the ELEPHANT or the HIPPOPOTAMOS would seem most evident from this consideration, that the TAIL of the LEVIATHAN or else the whole animal, is compared to a cedar of Lebanon. Now the tails of the elephant and hippopotamos are very insignificant in size, and are useless for defence or attack. Nor is there any apparent similitude between either of these animals and the stately cedar of Lebanon. Again, BEHEMOTH is described as "THE CHIEF OF THE WAYS OF GOD," which seems identical with the description of LEVIATHAN:

"There is not upon earth his like,
This creature without fear.
He looketh down on all that are exalted,
He the king over all the sons of pride."

It is difficult to imagine how these two passages can be predicated of any than of one and the same animal. Two reasons may be assigned why BEHEMOTH cannot signify an extinct saurian: I. Such saurian must have been as much unknown to Job as to us, and therefore the description could convey no conviction to his mind. II. The fossil remains of saurians which have been excavated exhibit no such tails as answer to the description, or in any way resemble the cedar of Lebanon. I advocate the conclusion, that BEHEMOTH and LEVIATHAN are two names, both designating the CROCODILE, and that these two names are given to this amphibious reptile on account of its twofold nature, terrestrial and aquatic—BEHEMOTH to indicate its superiority over all terrestrial animals, and LEVIATHAN to indicate its superiority over all aquatic animals. Crocodiles have been stated to measure in extreme length above fifty feet, French measure, between fifty and sixty feet English. The tail is about one-third the length of the whole animal, or about one-half the length measuring from its haunches, and is a most formidable weapon,—in the water overthrowing boats and canoes, and on land prostrating every living thing within its enormous sweep. I am ignorant what similitude can possibly exist between an animal and a cedar, except that the length of the one corresponds with the height of the other. Now the height of the tallest cedar is reported to be between seventy and eighty feet. Hence we may safely estimate the height of ordinary cedars to be between fifty and sixty feet, a close approximation to the measure of the largest crocodiles. We must also bear in mind that, since the invention of gunpowder, and more especially on account of the great increase and expansion of the human race, crocodiles have diminished in number, in range, and in size. I subjoin extracts from a few authorities to substantiate these statements.

"For four months crocodiles eat nothing. They are four-footed and amphibious. They deposit their eggs on the land, and leave them. The greater part of the day they pass on land, but the whole of the night in the river, because the water is warmer than the air and the dew. Of all animals with which we are acquainted, from the smallest beginning they attain the greatest size. Their eggs are little larger than those of geese, and the young are in proportion to the size of the eggs. But they grow to the length of seventeen cubits, and SOME TO A GREATER SIZE. They have the eyes of the boar. Their teeth are large and tusk-like in proportion to their mouth. Of all animals, they alone have no tongue."—*Herodotus.*

"Entre les animaux particulières à l'Egypte, il ne faut oublier les crocodiles, qui sont très-abondans dans le Nil, particulièrement dans la partie la plus méridionale du Said, et vers les cataractes. La ils fourmillent comme des vers dans les eaux de fleuve et entre les rochers qui forment les cataractes. Il y en a de grands et de petits, on en voit qui ont jusqu'à vingt condées de long."—*Abd-Allatif,* traduit par Baron de Sacy.

"J'ai vu à l'hospice de Négaudé la dépouille d'un crocodile de trent pieds de long, par quatre de largeur. L'ON M'A ASSURÉ QUIL SE'N TROUVOIT DANS LE NIL QUI AVOIENT JUSQU'A CINQUANTE PIEDS DE LONGUEUR."—*Sonnini.*

"Captain Norden saw, in Upper Egypt, twenty crocodiles extended on banks of sand in the Nile. They were, he says, of different sizes, namely, FROM FIFTEEN TO FIFTY FEET."—*Scott.*

"The crocodile, though not so powerful as in the water, is yet very terrible even upon land. It seldom, except when pressed with hunger, or with a view of depositing its eggs, leaves the water. Its usual method is to float along upon the surface, and seize whatever animal comes within its reach; but when this method fails, it then goes closer to the bank. Disappointed of its fishy prey, it then waits, covered up among the sedges, in patient expectation of some land animal that comes to drink,—the dog, the bull, the tiger, or man himself. Nothing is seen of the insidious destroyer as the animal approaches, nor is its retreat discovered till it is too late for safety. It seizes its victim with a spring, and goes at a bound much faster than so unwieldy an animal could be thought capable of; then, having secured the creature with both teeth and claws, it drags it into the water, and instantly sinks with it to the bottom, and in this manner quickly drowns it. The crocodile seizes and destroys all animals, and is dreaded by all. ITS PRINCIPAL INSTRUMENT OF DESTRUCTION IS THE TAIL. With a single blow of this it has often overturned a canoe, and seized upon the poor savage, its conductor."—*Buffon.*

"The power, hideousness, treachery, and ferocity of the crocodile sufficiently justify the impersonation of Isaiah xxvii. 1. Leviathan the piercing serpent—leviathan the crooked serpent—the dragon that is in the sea."—Fairbairn's *Bible Dictionary.*

VER. 14. *The rows of his teeth are terrific.*—"The opening of the mouth is of great width, and exhibits somewhat of a flexuous outline. Both jaws are covered with numerous sharp-pointed teeth. Each jaw contains thirty teeth or more. Their disposition is such, that when the mouth is shut, they alternate with each other."—*Anonymous author,* quoted by Fry. - "The crocodile has a single row of teeth in each jaw, implanted in sockets, from which they are reproduced when lost or broken. It has no lips, so that the teeth present a formidable appearance."—Tristram's *Natural History.*

VER. 18. *His eyes resemble the glancings of the dawn.*—"This has reference not to their peculiar brilliance, but to their position in the head. The crocodile's head is so formed, that its highest points are the eyes, and when it rises obliquely to the surface, the eyes are the first part of the whole animal to emerge. The Egyptians observing this, compared it to the sun rising out of the sea, and made it the hieroglyphic representative of the idea of sunrise." —Fairbairn's *Bible Dictionary.*

VER. 31. *Odoriferous as perfume.*—" On trouve à la surface du corps du crocodile, vers la région du ventre, une tumeur de grosseur d'un œuf, qui contient une substance humide de la nature du sang. Cette tumeur ressemble pour la forme et pour l'odeur à une vessie de musc. Je sais d'une personne digne de foi, qu'il s'en rencontre quelquefois, quoique rarement, qui ne le cèdent en rien au musc pour la force de l'odeur."—*Abd-Allatif,* traduit par Baron de Sacy.

" Les vieux crocodiles ont sous l'aisselle un follicule de la grosseur d'une noisette, dans lequel est une matière épaisse qui a l'odeur du musc. Les Egyptiens ont soin de l'enlever lorsquils tuent un crocodile, parce que ce parfum est fort estimé des grands du pays."—*Hasselquist.*

CHAP. XL. VER. 15 to CHAP. XLI. VER. 34.—" Man, as originally created, was invested with supreme dominion over all the creatures. But that original grant was greatly impaired by the Fall, and his inferiority to the creatures, wherever he is inferior to them, is a consequence of the Fall. Even in a literal sense, therefore, this reference to behemoth and leviathan is connected with man's degeneracy consequent on sin."—*Bishop Wordsworth.*

FIRST REPLY OF JOB TO JEHOVAH.

CHAPTER XLII.—VERSES 1-6.

Job acknowledgeth the sovereignty of Jehovah, expresseth contrition and godly sorrow, and anxiously inquires why he was thus afflicted.

1 Then Job answered Jehovah, and said :

2 I know that Thou canst do all things,
  And that no purpose of Thine can be frustrated.

3 " Who is this (sayest Thou) that darkeneth counsel
  By words without knowledge ?"

  Therefore have I uttered what I understood not,
  Things too wonderful for me which I knew not.

4 Hear now, I beseech Thee, and let me speak ;
  Let me ask of Thee, and do Thou inform me.

5 I have heard Thee with the hearing of the ear,
  But now mine eye hath seen Thee.

6 Wherefore am I become loathsome,
  And am scorched up upon dust and ashes?

Rightful position of XLII. 1-6 *before* XLI. 1-14.—Three reasons may be assigned for this rectification of the transposition existing in the Authorized Version, namely, placing xlii. 1-6 before xli. 1-14. Firstly, xli. 1-14 in the Authorized Version interrupts the regular order of the speech of Jehovah, and intervenes between the description of the eagle and of behemoth. Secondly, according to the order of our Version, and interpretation of the Hebrew, Job proposes to ask a question, xlii. 4, " I will demand of Thee, and declare Thou unto me;" and God answers the question, xl. 2, " Shall he that contendeth with the Almighty instruct Him? He that reproveth God, let him answer it," and yet no question by Job appears in our Version. Thirdly, the first hemistich of xlii. 6 cannot signify by any possibility, " Wherefore I abhor myself." Schultens renders it as Kennicott has done: " propterea contabescam porro in ulceribus meis," " Wherefore am I become loathsome?" The preceding verb, שאל (let me ask of Thee), gives an interrogative sense to verse 6.—See *Heath.*

"Let us proceed to the general difficulty, which arises at present from Job's confession in xlii. 6 : 'I abhor myself, and repent in dust and ashes.' But *repent* of what? and why *abhor himself?* He was, at that instant, in the very situation he had been earnestly wishing, and often praying for; and was it possible for him not to seize that favourable moment? What he had so often wished was, that God would appear, and permit him to ask the reason of his uncommon sufferings. See x. 2, xiii. 3 and 18-23, xix. 7, xxiii. 3-10, xxxi. 35-37. And now when God does appear, we see that Job, immediately attentive to this matter, resolves to put the question, and declares this resolution—' Hear, I beseech Thee, and I will speak : I will demand of Thee, and declare Thou unto me. I have heard of Thee by the hearing of the ear, but now mine eye seeth Thee.' What now becomes of Job's question? Does he put any? Far at present are the next words from any such meaning, at least in our present Version : for there the verse expresses nothing but sorrow for sin, which sets the poem at variance with itself: it also loses all sight of the question, for which the poem had been prepared, and which Job himself declares he would now put! Add, that in the first of these two lines the verb does not signify, I ABHOR MYSELF. So many verses as would fill one piece of vellum in an ancient roll might be easily sewed in before or after its proper place. In the case before us, the twenty-five lines in the first fourteen verses of chapter xl. seem to have been sewed in improperly after xxxix. 30, instead of after xlii. 6. That such large parts have been thus transposed in rolls (to make which the parts were sewed together) is absolutely certain ; see my Second Dissertation, pages 342, 572, and Dissertation Generalis, page 72."—Kennicott's *Posthumous Remarks on Select Passages in the Old Testament*—a book little known, but essential to the critical study of the Old Testament Scriptures.

SECOND ADDRESS OF JEHOVAH TO JOB.

CHAPTER XL.—VERSES 1, 2.

Jehovah refuseth to answer the question of Job.

1 Then Jehovah answered Job, and said :

2 Will contention with the Almighty rectify this?
  Let him that impleadeth God reply.

SECOND REPLY OF JOB TO JEHOVAH.

CHAPTER XL.—VERSES 3-5.

Job penitentially confesses his innate sinfulness, acknowledgeth his inability to answer God, and avows implicit submission to His will.

3 Then Job answered Jehovah, and said :

4 Behold, I am vile, what can I answer Thee ?
   I lay my hand upon my mouth.

5 Once have I spoken, but I will not reply again ;
   Yea, a second time (I now speak), but will add no more.

THIRD ADDRESS OF JEHOVAH TO JOB.

CHAPTER XL.—VERSES 6-14.

Jehovah closes the controversy by reiterating His perfections of sovereignty and omnipotence, that Job might deduce therefrom the duty of implicit subordination to the will of Him who doeth all things well. Though no solution is EXPLICITLY *given of the mystery why God permitted Satan to buffet Job, yet one design thereof is plainly implied, namely, to humble the patriarch in the dust, to strip him of all self-righteousness and self-confidence, and to bring him to a simple dependence on the love and covenant mercies of God for salvation from all his trials.*

   TO HUMBLE THE SINNER, EXALT THE SAVIOUR, AND PROMOTE HOLINESS OF LIFE, *is the primary lesson inculcated in this Poem, and in all the other books of Divine revelation.*

6 Then Jehovah answered Job
   Out of the whirlwind, and said :

7 Gird up now thy loins like a man,
   And I will question thee, and inform thou Me.

8 Wilt thou indeed disannul My judgment ?
   Wilt thou condemn Me, that thou mayest be justified ?

9 Hast thou indeed an arm like God ?
   And canst thou thunder with a voice like His ?

10 Deck thyself now with dignity and state,
    And robe thyself with majesty and glory.

11 Pour out the ebullitions of thy wrath,
    And eye every proud man and abase him.

12 Eye every proud man and fell him,
    Yea, crush down the malefactors to their grave.

13 Bury them in the dust together,
    Bandage their faces in their burying-place.

14 Then I, even I, will confess to thee,
    That thine own right hand can save thee.

CHAP. XL. VER. 13. *Bury—Burying-place.*—The imagery is taken from the Oriental custom of depositing their grain in motamores, or subterraneous granaries, whereby the buried produce of their harvests is not only concealed from the enemy in the event of invasion, but is preserved in greater security and perfection than it would be in our barns and above-ground receptacles of corn. The Saxon terms BURY and BURIAL-PLACE exactly correspond with the Hebrew verb and noun employed in this verse.

THE EPILOGUE.

CHAPTER XLII.—VERSES 7-17.

Jehovah rebukes Eliphaz, Bildad, and Zophar, because they had not spoken penitentially and submissively unto Him, as Job had finally spoken at the termination of the controversy. He commands them to offer sacrifices for the sins they had committed, and to seek the intercession of Job on their behalf.

Job is delivered from all his trials, and is restored to prosperity twofold greater than what he had heretofore possessed. Job died in faith, in a good old age, satiated with life, and willing to depart and be with that Redeemer, of whom he had prophesied, and in whom he had believed to the salvation of his soul. Like Abraham, "he looked for a city that hath foundations, whose builder and maker is God" (HEBREWS xi. 10).

7 Now, it came to pass after Jehovah had spoken
   These self-same words unto Job,
   That Jehovah said to Eliphaz the Temanite,
   " Enkindled is My anger against thee,
   And against thy two companions,
   Because ye have not spoken unto Me that which is right,
   As hath my servant Job.

8 Now therefore take for yourselves
   Seven bullocks and seven rams,
   And go ye unto my servant Job,
   And offer for yourselves a burnt-offering,

And my servant Job shall intercede for you,
For to him I will have regard,
That I visit not upon you your folly,
Because ye have not spoken unto Me that which is right,
As hath my servant Job."
9 Then went Eliphaz the Temanite,
And Bildad the Shuhite, and Zophar the Naamathite,
And did as Jehovah had spoken unto them.

And Jehovah had regard to Job,
10 And Jehovah reversed the captivity of Job
After he had made intercession for his friends,
And increased twofold all that had pertained to Job.
11 Then came unto him all his brethren,
And all his sisters, and all who before had known him,
And ate bread with him in his house,
And condoled with him and comforted him
Over all the evil which Jehovah had brought upon him.
And every one presented to him one kesita,
And every one one ring of gold.
12 So Jehovah blessed the latter end of Job
More than his beginning.
For to him pertained fourteen thousand sheep,
And six thousand camels,
A thousand yoke of oxen,
And a thousand she-asses.
13 And seven sons had he, and three daughters,
14 And he called the name of the first Jemima (Turtle-dove),
And the name of the second Kezia (Cassia),
And the name of the third Keren-happuch (Cornucopia),
15 And in all the land were no women found
So beautiful as the daughters of Job.
And their father gave to them
An inheritance in the midst of their brethren.
16 And Job lived after this
One hundred and forty years,
And saw his sons, and son's sons,
Four generations.
Then died Job old and satisfied with days.

CHAP. XLII. VERS. 7, 8. *Ye have not spoken unto Me that which is right, as hath my servant Job.*—The rendering of the Authorized Version both in verses 7 and 8 is : "YE HAVE not spoken OF ME." In the whole compass of the Hebrew Scriptures, the original, to the best of my knowledge, is never translated OF ME elsewhere than in these verses, nor will the original bear this acceptation. "Is, AD quem verba facimus quemque alloquimur, ponitur plerumque prævio אֶל."—Gesenii *Thesaurus Linguæ Hebrææ*. The rendering of the Authorized Version limits the Divine approbation bestowed upon Job, and the Divine censure upon Eliphaz, Bildad, and Zophar, to their argumentation detailed from chapter iii. to the end of chapter xxxi. This cannot be correct. For out of the whirlwind Jehovah said to Job, in censure, not in approbation, concerning his part in the argument :

"Who is this that darkeneth counsel
By words without knowledge?"

The rendering UNTO ME, adopted in this volume, restricts the Divine approbation upon Job to the last words he is recorded to have spoken :

"Behold, I am vile, what can I answer Thee?
I lay my hand upon my mouth.
Once have I spoken, but I will not reply again ;
Yea, a second time (I now speak), but will add no more."

Now, what do these words of Job imply? They are, firstly, a confession of inborn and inherent sin, of innate sinfulness, original and actual. They are, secondly, a protestation of implicit submission to the sovereignty of Jehovah in grace and providence. God's anger was kindled against Eliphaz, Bildad, and Zophar, because they had not, like Job, humiliated themselves before Jehovah, after He had spoken in the whirlwind, because they had not confessed to God their innate vileness, when Job confessed his vileness, nor acknowledged the Divine sovereignty, at the time when Job, His servant, had so acknowledged. "The expression rendered 'ye have not spoken of Me,' is never used as speaking OF, or CONCERNING, or BEFORE, but uniformly of speaking TO, or addressing a person, and consequently, in this passage, can only refer to Job's humble address to the Almighty after his trial, which Eliphaz, Bildad, and Zophar had omitted; though, in the eyes of the Omniscient, it behoved them to make the same confession. The construction of the Hebrew phrase is, perhaps, one of the most frequently occurring in every part of the Hebrew Scriptures. And it is invariably to 'speak TO,' or address, so that not the least doubt can remain of this being its EXCLUSIVE meaning. See the beginning of this very verse, and chapters ii. 13, iv. 2, and wherever it is used in the Book of Job."—*Fry*. *My servant*, see note on i. 8.

VER. 10. *Reversed the captivity of Job.*—This is a paronomasia, a common idiomatic phrase in the East, employed to signify a change from adversity to prosperity, "a restoration from great affliction and misery to a happy state." So Schultens, Parkhurst, and Lee. But in this passage the phrase seems to embody a more recondite meaning. Satan had despoiled Job of his family and property, and inflicted upon him painful bodily disease, that he might tempt him to abandon the service and worship of Jehovah. The tempter afflicted his body that he might ruin his soul. He assailed him by the desertion of his family and friends, by the scathing invectives of Eliphaz, Bildad, and Zophar, and by the suggestion of evil thoughts to his soul, that he might make him captive to sin, and death, and hell. The liberation of Job was not only deliverance from secular suffering, but from afflictive temptation of soul. He who "led captivity captive, and received gifts for men, even for the rebellious, that the Lord God might dwell among them," now liberated both the soul and body of Job from Satan, and made Job more than conqueror through Him that loved him. He who manifested Himself to Abraham at Mamre, and to Jacob at Bethel, and was present in the burning bush in the wilderness, and in the pillar of fire and cloud, which for forty years regulated and guarded the encampments of Israel, was now present with Job by His indwelling Spirit until death was swallowed up in victory.

VER. 11. *A kesita.*—The antiquity of the Book of Job, written, we assume, before the Abrahamic period, peremptorily excludes all reference therein to coined money. Who can imagine that coined money could have been current in the East, while Noah and Shem and Eber were yet living? The most ancient coined money now extant is that of Lydia and Ægina. The most learned Numismatists do not assign these coins to an age earlier than the eighth or possibly the ninth century before Christ. "The use of coined money in Palestine cannot have existed till after the taking of Samaria by the Assyrians (in B.C. 721). The real meaning of

KESITA seems to be A PORTION, and it is evidently a piece of silver of unknown weight."—Madden's *Jewish Coinage*. "KESITA does not occur in the plural, and only thrice in the singular number, Genesis xxxiii. 19; Joshua xxiv. 32; and Job xlii. 11. It signifies a piece of money so called, consisting apparently of a certain WEIGHT of silver, as the word signifies something WEIGHED. From a comparison of Genesis xxxiii. 19 with Genesis xxiii. 15, 16, the KESITA would seem to be of the value of four shekels."—Lee's *Hebrew Lexicon*. As the kesita was a certain weight of silver, so it would seem that the ring of gold was not a nasal jewel, but rather a piece of ring-money, such as is represented in Wilkinson's *Ancient Egyptians*, vol. ii. p. 11.

VER. 14.—The names given by Job to his three daughters were emblematic. TURTLE-DOVE was emblematic of innocence and harmlessness. CASSIA, of aromatic fragrance. CORNU-COPIA, of the possession, and dotation to others, of plenty. JEMIMA, with a slight variation of the Rabbinic punctuation, is not only the Arabic term for a TURTLE-DOVE, but is also the appellation of an ancient lady or queen of Arabia, "celebrated for fine eyes and an acute sight" (Richardson's *Arabic Dictionary*), a tradition doubtless of Job's eldest daughter. CASSIA is a generic term, comprehending CINNAMON (the *Cinnamomum cassia* of botanists, the *Cinnamomum zeylanicum* of the British Pharmacopœia), and CASSIA (the koorst of the Arabs, costus of the ancients, the orris, or *Aucklandia costus* of botanists). KEREN-HAPPUCH literally signifies the HORN INVERTED. It has no reference to stibium or kohl, as rendered by many interpreters. The last syllable of this name, signifying stibium, occurs four times in the Hebrew Scriptures, but in all four passages it is an anarthrous noun. The prefix of what is the definite article in Hebrew to the last syllable of Keren-happuch proves that happuch is not a noun, but is the Pahul or past participle of the Hebrew verb signifying to TURN, INVERT, etc. There is no historic proof that painting the eyes was customary in Arabia in the days of Job, nor is it probable that this practice existed at so early a period. KEREN-HAPPUCH is rendered AMALTHÆA in the Coptic and LXX. Versions. This manifestly shows that those translators considered the term as synonymous with PLENTY. The inversion of the horn evidently implies the dotation of that plenty to others. In the geography of Arabia and the neighbouring countries it is easy to trace places named after each of the three daughters of Job, and retaining the names originally given to them, after the lapse of above 4100 years.

1*st*, Jemimah is the name of a region in Arabia, so called after the Lady or Queen of Arabia above named; 2*d*, of a province in Arabia; 3*d*, of land called Jemama in Arabia; 4*th*, of a river abounding with excellent fish (Castell's *Heptaglott Lexicon*). A central province in Arabia called Yemáma is mentioned by the Arabian geographer Ebn Haukal, and occurs prominently in Palgrave's Map of Arabia. "The name of the eldest daughter, Jemima, stands so accurately represented by that of Jemima or Jemama, the central province of the Arabian peninsula, that (the known origin of most names of localities in Arabia considered) the evidence of the probable derivation would be good, did it rest on the coincidence of name alone. In the instance of the province of Jemama, however, it so fortunately happens that we possess the wholly independent evidence of native tradition as to the territorial appellation having had its origin in a FEMALE PROPER NAME. The historical fact, that some kingdoms of Arabia were anciently governed by female sovereigns, is familiar to all. The province of JEMAMA is specially mentioned by the Arabs themselves as an example in point, and (without the most distant reference to the daughter of Job) an Arab tradition of immemorial standing has preserved and handed down to us the further fact, that this province originally derived its name JEMAMA (or the dove) from QUEEN JEMAMA, the first sovereign of the land. That this ancient Arab queen was no other than JEMIMA, the eldest daughter of Job, is a conclusion natural in itself, conformable with the analogy of the patriarchal blessings, and confirmed by the ascertained existence, in or near the land of Uz, of a people named the Agubeni, Beni Ayub, or sons of Job."—Forster's *Geography of Arabia*, quoted by Carey.

2. Besides some places, respecting which doubts may be entertained, KEZIA seems to have been the origin of the name KHUZISTAN, a country to the north of the Persian Gulf, called in Latin SUSIANNA.

3. The Arabic قرن, the first section of the name KEREN-HAPPUCH, is the name of—1*st*, a town in Jemamah; 2*d*, of a city; 3*d*, of a mountain; and 4*th*, in the dual number, of two mountains in Jemamah (Castell's *Heptaglott Lexicon*). It is the name of a town KARUN, or KAROON, situated on the bank of a river of the same name, which empties itself eastward into the Shatt-el-Arab, and is so denominated in the maps of Chesney and Palgrave. It is also identical with Kurnah or Kurnah, a town situated at the junction of the rivers Tigris

and Euphrates, to the north of the Shatt-el-Arab. See maps of Niebuhr, Chesney, and Palgrave.

Thus the daughters of Job seem to have called after their own names the lands granted to them by their father Job for an inheritance among their brethren. After the lapse of above 4100 years, several of these lands are now known and described by the self-same names of Job's daughters, whose patrimony they were, and after whose names they were called. This is an irrefragable proof that Job, Eliphaz, Bildad, Zophar, Jemima, Kezia, and Keren-happuch were real personages, and that this Book from beginning to end is historically true, and not a drama or fiction, as infidelity impiously assumes.

VER. 16. *Satisfied with days.*—The Syriac and Arabic Versions render "*satisfied with days*, SATURATUS DIEBUS SUIS." "Satisfied with days or living, 'CONVIVA SATUR,' as Horace expresses it, and before him Lucretius, 'PLENUS VITÆ CONVIVA.' So Seneca, 'vixi, Lucilli charissime, quantum satis est, mortem plenus expecto.'"—Parkhurst's *Hebrew Lexicon.* Job had experienced the extreme both of prosperity and adversity. He had suffered all which the malignity of Satan could inflict, and had subsequently realized all the enjoyment this world can afford. By sanctified affliction he was stripped of all self-righteousness and self-confidence, and attained to the full assurance of faith, hope, and understanding. The Spirit bare witness to his spirit, that all his sins had been forgiven ; that he had passed from death unto life ; that he had perfect justification and acceptance with God. Therefore, in the plenitude of faith he wished to die, and be present with that Messiah, of whom, as Redeemer and Mediator, he had prophesied. He was anxious to be absent from the body, and present with the Lord. In his death was verified the prophetic anticipation of Eliphaz :—

"In ripe old age shalt thou come to the grave,
As the oblation of a shock of corn in its season."

Job, instated in the everlasting covenant in all things ordered and sure, died at that time, in that manner, and under those circumstances, which Jehovah from all eternity had ordained in love. Death separated him from his living family, and reunited him with his ten deceased children, from whom for years he had been dissociated by the machinations of Satan. Having by faith served God in his day and generation, and having been made more than conqueror through Him that loved him, he now by death entered into that rest, which remaineth to the people of God. Death translated Job, satiated with this world of sin and sorrow, from the church militant to the church triumphant, to the elect of the Father, the redeemed of the Son, and the sanctified of the Holy Ghost, to "the general assembly and church of the first-born, which are written in heaven" (*Hebrews* xii. 23). "Blessed are they who (like Job) wash their robes, that they may have right to the tree of life, and may enter in through the gates into the city" (*Revelation* xxii. 14).

CRITICAL APPENDIX.

"INTER omnia Sacri Codicis Monumenta exstare quodammodo mihi videtur Liber Jobi, quasi singulare quoddam atque unicum ; utpote minimam omnium cum cæteris habens cognationem, nullam cum Israelitarum rebus necessitudinem. Ponitur in Idumæâ scena Historiæ ; hominis Idumæi casus narrantur ; qui loquentes inducuntur sunt omnes Idumæi, vel FINITIMI ARABES. Sermo est PURE HEBRÆUS, quanquam auctore, ut videtur, Idumæo ; nam omnes Abrahami posteros Israelitas, Idumæos, Arabas tum Keturæos, tum Ishmaelitas, communi linguâ diu usos fuisse veri est simillimum. Idumæos autem, ac speciatim Themanitas, sapientiæ fama claruisse, Jeremiæ atque Abdiæ prophetarum testimonio constat.

Ante legem latam eum vixisse probabiliter inferri potest ex eo sacrificii genere, quod Deo jubente offert, septem nimirum juvencos et septem arietes : quod in iis regionibus, ea ætate, nondum deleta inter gentes Creationis intra septem dies memoria, obtinuisse, Balaami Aramæi exemplo constat.

Videor mihi vere constituere posse, hujus Poematis Argumentum esse, Tertiam ultimamque Jobi tentationem ab Amicis criminantibus factam : cujus eventus est, primo Jobi æstus, indignatio, contumacia ; deinde animi sedatio, submissio, pœnitentia : Ejusdem autem præcipuum esse Finem ; Ut homines doceat, habita ratione tum humanæ corruptionis, ignorantiæ, et debilitatis, tum infinitæ Dei sapientiæ et immensæ Majestatis, suis viribus, suæ justitiæ, renuntiandum esse ; Deo fidem habendum, et cum summa humilitate et reverentia ei esse in omnibus submittendum. Illud autem diligenter imprimis animadversum velim : aliud plane Disputationis inter Jobum et amicos, aliud universi Poematis esse Argumentum : alium plane esse Poematis, alium Universæ Historiæ, finem. Nam quanquam is fit, quem dixi, Finis, id argumentum Poematis, nihilo tamen minus concedi potest Historiam universam simul sumptam proprie continere PATIENTIÆ SPECTATÆ EXEMPLAR ET PRÆMIUM. Si priorem Historiæ partem, si posteriorem, si utramque includis ; jam habes PATIENTIÆ IN MISERIIS OMNIBUS EXTERNIS FERENDIS SPECTATÆ, ET A DEO TANDEM AMPLISSIMIS PRÆMIIS AFFECTÆ, INSIGNE DOCUMENTUM.

Hoc Poema sane in suo genere est pulcherrimum et perfectissimum. Quæ enim potest concipi in ejusmodi argumento, difficili, et recondito, et ab omni actione abstracto, elegantior œconomia ? Quæ distributio ordinatior ? Quæ, quantum in tantis vetustatis tenebris cernere possumus, accuratior, et subtilior, et ad finem consequendum aptior, rerum deductio?"—Lowth, *De Sacra Poesi Hebraeorum.*

"Totius Poematis ea est puritas, elegantia, sublimitas, qua nihil majus perfectiusque in toto Hebraico codice superest. Nec in Arabicis, quod ad eam propius accedit, legi. Hoc poema auream ubique linguae Hebraicae aetatem spirat."—*Michaelis.*

CHAPTER I. 11.

אִם Dum, quum, quando.—Noldii *Heb. Part.*

CHAPTER II. 5.

אִם Dum, quum, quando.—Noldii *Heb. Part.*

CHAPTER III. 8.

The order of construction would be (כ) אררי העתידים יום ע(ו)רר לויתן

CHAPTER IX. 9.

Schultens interprets this verse: "QUI FECIT NOCTURNUM CIRCITOREM; SIDUS TORPIDUM, SIDUSQUE CALIDUM; ET PENETRALIA AUSTRI."

He interprets, from the Arabic, עש CIRCUIVIT, GYRAVIT NOCTU, and in the participle present, VICILEM NOCTURNUM, CIRCITOREM. And Castell renders, CIRCUMIVIT, OBIVIT NOCTU.

Schultens interprets כסיל FRIGUS, SEGNITIEM, TORPOREM, SIDUS TORPIDUM. Castell, SIDUS FRIGIDUM.

Schultens interprets כימה SIDUS CALIDUM GENITALE. Castell, SIDUS CALIDUM.

And Schultens adds: "Mihi tutissimum videtur, ut כסיל complectatur SIDERA FRIGIDA ET BRUMALIA, כימה SIDERA CALORIS ET AESTATIS PRAENUNTIA."

And Schultens considers these three terms as opposed to PENETRALIBUS AUSTRI, id est, Haemispherio mundi nobis clauso, cujus SIDERA in conspectum nostrum nunquam emergunt, sed tanquam IN CONCLAVIBUS ET ABDITIS PENETRALIBUS DELITESCUNT.

CHAPTER XII. 6.

לאשר ל NEMPE, ID EST.—Noldii *Conc. Heb. Part.*

אלה אלוה is the reading of two Hebrew MSS. in Kennicott's *Hebrew Bible.*

CHAPTER XII. 18.

אזור SEMICINCTIUM SERVI.—Simonis *Lex. Heb.* See also Castell.

CHAPTER XII. 20.

נאמנים QUI PUBLICAE SECURITATI ET RERUM CUSTODIAE PRAESUNT, FIDENTIORES, PRINCIPES, MAGNATES, Arabicé.—Castell's *Lex. Heptagl.*

CHAPTER XIII. 1.

כל אלה is the reading of eighteen Hebrew MSS., Syriac, Vulgate, and Arabic.

Chapter xiv. 6.

רצה לָ‍, FIRMAVIT iv. INHÆSIT LOCO, MANSIT IN EO MINIME EXCEDENS.—Castell's *Lex. Heptagl.*

Chapter xiv. 8.

בְעֹפֶר ב SUPER, SUPRA.—Noldii *Conc. Heb. Part.*

Chapter xiv. 10.

וַיֵחֱלָשׁ HUMI STERNITUR.—Michaelis *Sup. ad Lex. Heb.*

Chapter xiv. 14.

HIMSELF ה HIC, ILLE.—Noldii *Conc. Heb. Part.*

Chapter xvii. 10.

כלכם is the reading of seven Hebrew MSS., Syriac, Arabic, and Vulgate.

Chapter xx. 4.

הלא is the reading of one of the oldest and best MSS. of De Rossi and of LXX.

Chapter xxi. 22.

"רמים VERMIBUS EROSUM. Non in form. plur. DE CELSIS, sed in sing. DE MORTUO A VERMIBUS EROSO, videtur interpretandum."—*Schultens.*

Chapter xxi. 33.

מתקן verbum præguans.

Chapter xxii. 18.

עצת the reading of one Hebrew MS.

Chapter xxii. 30.

אי—HABITATION.—Lee's *Heb. Lex.*
SETTLEMENT, HABITATION.—Parkhurst's *Heb. Lex.*
RESIDING IN ANY PLACE BY DAY OR NIGHT.—Richardson's *Arabic Lex.*

Chapter xxiii. 9.

شَعَ‍ SCRUTATUS FUIT, INQUISIVIT, EXTENDIT MANUM AD ALIQUID UT CAPERET vi. AVIDE EXPETIVIT REM.—Castell's *Lex. Heptagl.* See also note and version of Good.

Chapter xxiv. 18-25.

Verse 18. "Eæ deinceps tenebræ incumbent, quæ vix dispicere sinant, nedum dijudicare, aut certos gressus figere. Non nimium dixit certe Cler. quum hac periodo se obscurius quicquam in S. Script. novisse negat. Arguet obscuritatem istam incredibilis interpretationum dissonantia, quæ nuspiam major, molestior, distractior, dissipatiorque adeo. Utinam aliquid lucis ex discussione, quam capessimus, emicaret, ad periodum, excellentibus figuris, insignem rite constituendam. Id nobis successurum exigua, ac nulla potius, spes—Post longum cursum ancoram nuspiam adhuc jactare liceat; sed nova nobis pericula maris undosi maneant adeunda.

Verse 19. Non minores fluctus cymbulam huc illuc circumactam accipient—novæ iterum undæ nos in altum retrahunt; atque judicium suspendere cogunt.

Verse 21. Scindunt se viæ, sententiæque; et novis nos curis distrahunt huc illuc.

Verse 23. Eadem inconstantia, et jactatio, nos implicabit.

Verse 24. Omnia hæc arguunt contextus nostri obscuritatem cum ambiguitate omnium locutionum conjunctam.

Verse 25. Ad istam cynosuram navigandum inter has Syrtes, si quis portum contingere velit. Me quidem cum tenuisse haud certus sum : quin nimis vereor ne navim confregisse judicer, undis decumanis oppressus et abreptus."—*Schultens.*

CHAPTER XXIV. 24.

تفز and نفس mortuus fuit.—Castell's *Lex. Heptagl.* See also Fry *on Job.*

CHAPTER XXIV. 25.

QUOD SI NON ITA EST.—Noldii *Conc. Heb. Part.*

CHAPTER XXV. 2.

Castell interprets שלומים RETRIBUTIONES in Isaiah i. 23. See also Michaelis *Sup. ad Lex. Heb.*, Miss Smith, and Fry *on Job.*

CHAPTER XXV. 5.

ולא. The ו is omitted in fifty-three Hebrew MSS., ten editions Chaldee, Vulgate, Syriac, and Arabic.

CHAPTER XXVIII. 8.

ולא עדה is the reading of many Hebrew MSS., and three ancient editions.

CHAPTER XXVIII. 28.

No fewer than 108 Hebrew MSS. and Edd. read יהוה instead of אדני according to Kennicott's *Hebrew Bible,* and De Rossi gives " plurimi MSS. cum plerisque editionibus antiquis " in addition to this number.

CHAPTER XXX. 20.

One Hebrew MS. and Vulgate add ולא to the second hemistich.

CHAPTER XXX. 24.

Vouchsafes.—لپى iv. obtulit munus quid ex itinere advenienti.—Castell's *Lex. Heptagl.*

CHAPTER XXX. 25.

An non ploro, tanquam qui gravatus die? contabescit anima mea tanquam qui egenus?—*Schultens.*

CHAPTER XXXI. 28.

This is one of the most obscure passages in the Book of Job. The last word of the verse presents the chief difficulty. I consider it the first person singular of the future tense of the Niphal conjugation of the verb חנן, *to have compassion* (see Jeremiah xxxii. 23), and the final ה to be, as Noldius expresses it, expletivum seu redundans. Or אנחנה may be the first person singular of the future tense Niphal of the root חנה, giving to that verb its signification of its cognate חנן. In either case the meaning will be similar and almost identical.

CHAPTER XXXI. 37.

קרב 5 conj. accessit ad Deum, cum propitiare sibi studuit victimâ.—Castell's *Lex. Heptagl.*

CHAPTER XXXIV. 31.

Act perversely—خبل corrupit, depravavit, perversè egit.—Michaelis and Castell's *Lex. Heptagl.*

CHAPTER XXXIV. 36.

כאנשי is the reading of four Hebrew MSS., and of the LXX.

CHAPTER XXXVI. 17.

מלא verbum prægnans.

CHAPTER XXXVI. 22.

The LXX. render מורה δυνάστης, and Buxtorff states : "Summus titulus est doctorum, penes quos summa judicandi et decidendi potestas, cui alii Rabbini et Magistri subditi sunt, et quem in rebus dubiis appellant."

CHAPTER XXXVII. 9.

See note ix. 9, also *Simonis Lex Heb.*, by Eichhorn, page 470, and Mason Good on *Job* ix. 9 and xxxvii. 9.

CHAPTER XXXVII. 19.

Arrayed in robes of darkness.—See *Reiske* and *Mason Good.*

CHAPTER XXXVIII. 10.

Appointed.—شبر Arabicè, SPITHAMIS DIMENSUS FUIT, DONAVIT, PRÆBUIT, MAGNIFICAVIT.—Castell's *Lex. Heptagl.*

CHAPTER XXXVIII. 14.

A robe of light.—לבוש in Chaldee and Samaritan signifies LUMEN, FLAMMA, see Castell's *Lex. Heptagl.*, and is here rendered as a verbum prægnans.

CHAPTER XXXVIII. 30.

Congealed.—לכד CONCREVIT, CONGELATUS EST.—Castell's *Lex. Heptagl.* Arabicè, INTER SE COHÆRENT, COMPACTA SUNT, in fifth conj., JUNCTIS INTER SE AUXIT ET COMPACTIS PARTIBUS FUIT.—Simonis *Lex. Heb.*, Eichhorn.

CHAPTER XXXVIII. 31, 32.

See notes on ix. 9. *Stellar attendants*, Michaelis in his *Sup. ad. Lex. Heb.* thus explains :—" Stella polaris, Arabica phrasi, possit recte MATER STELLARUM dici, quod est altissima. Hæc sola cum per totam noctem annique omne tempus, non in Syria solum ac Palestina, sed in Arabia, Ægyptoque, nunquam occidat, reliquis stellis occidentibus, et tanquam morientibus, matri comparari possit, filiis orbae, illisque superstiti."

Chapter XXXVIII. 37.

Irradiate.—أَضَاءَ ILLUXIT, IMMINUIT, fourth conj., ENITUIT, SPLENDUIT, RELUXIT.—Castell's *Lex. Heptagl.*

Chapter XXXIX. 5.

The brayer.—جَرَّ ELATIORE VOCE ET CUM CORPORIS MOTU RECIPROCATAM INFLEXIT VOCEM, Castell's *Lex. Heptagl.*, per onomatopœiam.

Chapter XXXIX. 18.

Speeds her course.—مَرَى AD VEHEMENTIOREM CURSUM SCUTICA ALIAVE EGIT EQUUM—ANTERIORES PEDES IN SOLO MOTITAVIT EQUUS PRÆ AGILITATE.—Castell's *Lex. Heptagl.*

Chapter XL. 17.

He brandishes (his tail).—حَفَضَ INFLEXIT, CONTORSITQUE.—Castell's *Lex. Heptagl.* יחפץ is the reading of thirty-seven Heb. MSS., and two ancient editions.

Chapter XL. 20.

Would be slaughtered.—سَحَق FRICANDO TRIVIT ET CONTRIVIT, COMMINUITVE IN PULVEREM, NECAVIT, vii. conj. CONTRITUS FUIT.—Castell's *Lex. Heptagl.*

Chapter XL. 24.

Roaring waves.—I derive מוקשים from the Arabic نَقَشَ SONUIT, RES. pec. INANIMATA, ut FRAGORE DOMUS, dum finderetur, CREPITU OSSA, SOLVIT, DISSOLVIT.—Castell's *Lex. Heptagl.* See also Fry's note.

Chapter XLI. 1 (XL. 25).

שׁקע, LIGAVIT, CINXIT, Heb. חבשׁ sam. LIGAVIT, ex usu sam. optime S. Hieron. Job xli. 1.—Castell's *Lex. Heptagl.*

Chapter XLI. 11 (XLI. 3).

תחת is an archaic substantive signifying SUBSTRATUM.

Chapter XLI. 12 (XLI. 4).

The version of this verse is taken from Lee, whose note is, "I feel compelled to take the Arabic حَين or حَون, PERIIT, EXITIUM, PERNICIES." So also Castell.

Chapter XLI. 30 (XLI. 22).

Sharp splinters.—SHARP-POINTED STONES.—*Coptic Version.*

Chapter XLI. 31 (XLI. 23).

Odoriferous.—The Hebrew verb in Syriac signifies ODORATUS EST.—Castell's *Lex. Heptagl.*

Chapter XLII. 9.

וצפר is the reading of forty-eight Hebrew MSS., LXX., Syriac, Vulgate, Arabic.

WORKS BY THE SAME AUTHOR.

Imperial 8vo, price Twelve Shillings.

PSALTERIUM MESSIANICUM DAVIDIS REGIS ET PROPHETÆ.

A REVISION OF THE

Authorized English Versions of the Book of Psalms,

WITH QUOTATIONS FROM PRE-REFORMATION WRITERS,

VINDICATING, IN ACCORDANCE WITH THE INTERPRETATION OF THE NEW TESTAMENT, DAVID'S PROPHETIC MANIFESTATION OF MESSIAH, THE ALPHA AND OMEGA, THE SHEPHERD, PROPHET, PRIEST, AND KING, THE PATTERN AND EXEMPLAR OF ALL THE BLOOD-BOUGHT SHEEP OF IMMANUEL, OF EVERY AGE AND OF EVERY CLIME.

"This is a most praiseworthy, laborious, and learned work. It has evidently been to the author a labour of love. The work bears marks of close, diligent, and reverential study throughout. The author is an excellent Hebraist, and has a thorough acquaintance with both patristic, mediaeval, and Reformation Theology."—*The Record.*

"In preparing his work, the author merits commendation for the labour which he has bestowed upon the collation of manuscripts, editions, and versions, and for his industry in collecting passages from many authors of all periods. On these accounts the volume will be useful to the critic and the expositor, who will find in it much curious matter worthy of attention."—*Journal of Sacred Literature.*

"The title of this valuable work is accurately indicative of its contents. To appreciate the excellence of this book, it must be not only read, but studied. The quotations from the writings of the ancient Christian and Jewish authors, with reference to the Psalms which Mr. Coleman views as prophetical of the future exaltation of Christ in the Millennial kingdom, and of the events by which its establishment is to be preceded, are intensely interesting. The work is beautifully printed in a large and clear type."—*Achill Missionary Herald.*

"A very valuable edition of the Psalms, PROVING, that which has long been with us a settled conviction, that they are all Messianic."—*The Rainbow.*

LONDON: JAMES NISBET AND CO., 1865.

Post 8vo, price Seven Shillings and Sixpence.

A MEMOIR OF THE REV. RICHARD DAVIS,

FOR THIRTY-NINE YEARS A MISSIONARY IN NEW ZEALAND.

"Hitherto we have had but little in the way of authorship from New Zealand, and nothing that has appeared, for fulness, variety, and completeness of information, is for a moment to be compared with this well-filled volume. It does for New Zealand, already an interesting colony, and destined to occupy a chief place in the south, what the missionary enterprises of John Williams did for the groups of which he treated. It is thoroughly a missionary work, and a great addition to the missionary library."—Dr. Campbell's *British Standard.*

Imperial 8vo, price Five Shillings.

ECCLESIASTES.

A New Translation.

WITH NOTES EXPLANATORY, ILLUSTRATIVE, AND CRITICAL.

"The deviations of this translation in many instances yield a better meaning, or express the meaning with more perspicuity than our English Version. The translation is arranged in parallel lines, which not only exhibit to the eye the peculiar characteristic of Hebrew poetry, but render the meaning and point of this didactic poem the more obvious. The explanatory notes often solve what is difficult and obscure in the book, throw light on the reign and character of Solomon, and bring out clearly and impressively his deep repentance for the sins he had committed."—*British and Foreign Evangelical Review.*

"We recommend this work to our readers, as combining with much originality, sound sense, sound philosophy, and lastly, what in these days is no small excellence, the sound Protestantism of of the sixteenth century."—*Achill Missionary Herald.*

LONDON: JAMES NISBET AND CO., 1867.

www.ingramcontent.com/pod-product-compliance
Lightning Source LLC
Chambersburg PA
CBHW020058170426
43199CB00009B/319